Casey and Diana

Nick Green

Casey and Diana
first published 2024 by Scirocco Drama
An imprint of J. Gordon Shillingford Publishing Inc.
© 2024 Nick Green

Scirocco Drama Editor: Glenda MacFarlane
Cover design by Doowah Design
Author photo by Ryan Parker Photography
Production photos by Cylla Von Tiedemann.
Photo of Casey House courtesy of the Casey House Collection.

Printed and bound in Canada on 100% post-consumer recycled paper.

Production inquiries to:
Colin Rivers, Marquis Entertainment
www.MQlit.ca
colin@MQent.ca

Library and Archives Canada Cataloguing in Publication

Title: Casey and Diana / Nick Green.
Names: Green, Nick (Playwright), author.
Identifiers: Canadiana 20240358147 | ISBN 9781990738319 (softcover)
Subjects: LCGFT: Drama.
Classification: LCC PS8613.R42825 C37 2024 | DDC C812/.6—dc23

We acknowledge the financial support of the Canada Council for the Arts, the Government of Canada, the Manitoba Arts Council, and the Manitoba Government for our publishing program

Canada Council   Conseil des arts   Funded by the   **Canada**   MANITOBA   CONSEIL DES ARTS   **Manitoba**
for the Arts   du Canada   Government   ARTS COUNCIL DU MANITOBA
                                    of Canada

J. Gordon Shillingford Publishing
P.O. Box 86, RPO Corydon Avenue, Winnipeg, MB Canada R3M 3S3

Nick Green

Nick Green is a Dora Mavor Moore, Elizabeth Sterling Haynes, and Tom Hendry Award-winning playwright based in Toronto. Featured writing credits include: *Casey and Diana* (Stratford Festival of Canada and Soulpepper Theatre); *In Real Life* (book, Musical Stage Company, Tom Hendry Award Winner); *Dr. Silver* (book, South Coast Repertory's Pacific Playwrights Festival 2022 and 2023); *Every Day She Rose* (co-written with Andrea Scott, Nightwood Theatre); *Happy Birthday Baby J* (Shadow Theatre); *Dinner with the Duchess* (Next Stage); *Body Politic* (lemonTree Creations/Buddies in Bad Times, Dora Mavor Moore Award Winner, Outstanding New Play); *Fangirl* (book, Musical Stage Company); *Living the Dream* (book, Canadian Music Theatre Projects); *Poof! The Musical* (book, Twenties Street Productions, Elizabeth Sterling Haynes Award Nomination); and *Coffee Dad, Chicken Mom, and the Fabulous Buddha Boi* (Guys in Disguise, winner of three Elizabeth Sterling Haynes Awards).

Nick has been a part of the Foerster Bernstein New Play Development Program at the Stratford Festival of Canada; Factory Theatre's Natural Resources Unit; Nightwood Theatre's Write from the Hip development program; and Theatre Sheridan's Canadian Music Theatre Project.

During the pandemic, Nick was the creator and director of The Social Distancing Festival, an online exhibition of international art. This festival was recognized and acclaimed by publications that include the *New York Times*, the CBC, the BBC, the *Guardian*, *The Hindu*, *Time Out Dubai*, Radio Berlin, and more. The Social Distancing Festival website was archived from 2020 to 2023 by the United States Library of Congress and inducted into their collection.

Playwright's Note

There are seven things I want to say to you at the start of this play:

1) *Casey and Diana* is a play that is about capacity. I mean this in two ways: the ability and/or potential that people have to be kind, to give, and to learn; and the amount that a single person can hold without breaking, overflowing, exploding, disintegrating, etc. Capacity grows when fed a diet of compassion, forgiveness, and patience.

2) "Great consideration for one another, that's what's going to save the world." Casey House Founder June Callwood.

3) There was a time that happened to be my 40th birthday when I was doing a talkback in Stratford's Studio Theatre after a matinee that was attended by a big group of people associated with Casey House, including founders, nurses and staff, volunteers, and folks who had lost loved ones, and when we were talking about Diana's visit, one woman shared that she had been there that day, at which point another woman across the theatre — on the other side of the thrust stage — said that she remembered seeing her at Casey House on that day, and they reconnected and there was this great, energetic line, like a lightning bolt, that shot across the

stage, tying together the past and present, the imagined and the real, that made me feel very grateful for the profound connection that comes from the mix of community and art.

4) The character of Thomas is written as someone who's bald, but I'm okay with talking about adjusting that if you're producing this play and have a really great actor in mind who has a full head of hair. I mean, they could shave their head, but I wouldn't want anyone doing that if they don't want to. Or worse, wearing a bald cap.

5) In the end, once you've exhaled and you're dead, all that's left of you is the impact you've had on other people. Give wisely, because what you give is immortal.

6) When I started this project, I committed to infusing love into its creation; into all the words, all the drafts, the editing, the research, love love love. When I brought it to Bob White, he treated the idea and early drafts with great love. When I met with Joanne and Lisa at Casey House, they greeted me with warmth and love. When Andrew Kushnir came on board and became my biggest advocate and collaborator, I felt incredible love. When my agent, Colin Rivers, helped me dream-big-blue-sky-you-can-do-it, he did it with the most love, as always. When the Stratford Festival kept giving more support, and I began to be embraced by all the incredible people in that company, I felt swept up by love. There was love in the workshops and love in the feedback and questions. Love in the interviews with those connected to the true story. Love in the COVID setbacks and love in the Zoom rooms. Love from my family as I kept creating. On the first day of rehearsals for the Stratford Festival production, I asked the company to channel the spirit of Casey House

throughout the process by bringing love to the work. The love of the cast, the stage managers, the designers, the technical teams and producers and communication teams and ushers and everyone has been incredible and moving and so, so apparent all along the way. It has been wonderful and perfect, and I am grateful.

7) When a play is created from a place of love, any success that play might find is then, of course, the direct result of love.

Nick Green
Spring 2024

Foreword

Welcome to the extraordinary tale of *Casey and Diana*, a play that shares the remarkable story of compassion, resilience, and the indomitable spirit of a community brought together in a crisis of health, stigma and shame. This play celebrates the legacy of an organization that has been a beacon of radical kindness for over thirty-five years.

In the early years of Casey House, the seeds of radical kindness were sown and nurtured by a commitment to unequivocal compassion. This value, born from the belief that every individual deserves care and dignity, became the DNA of Casey House. Through Nick Green's telling of Princess Diana's visit, the reader embarks on a journey that traces the roots of this compassionate movement, one that was honoured by a Princess and has continued to flourish in the organization's present. As expressed by Nancy Lucier, the daughter of a client who died at Casey House in 1991, "Princess Diana's visit carried my family and I through a very difficult time at the height of the [AIDS] pandemic. Princess Diana's visit played such an important part of our story. It changed our whole journey."

In the pivotal year of 1988, when Casey House opened its doors, the AIDS crisis had reached its zenith, marked by soaring incidence rates, an absence of viable treatment options, and a pervasive atmosphere of stigma and discrimination.

In the early years, the stark reality of a nine-month average life expectancy for those living with AIDS underscored the urgency of our mission. In a society steeped in stigma, many faced isolation in their final moments, severed from familial, social, and medical support. Driven by an unwavering belief in the dignity of dying according to one's own wishes and the profound need for love and compassion in that journey, June Callwood, lead founder of Casey House, envisioned a sanctuary of both medical excellence and unwavering warmth.

As our first client crossed the threshold, a simple yet profound gesture encapsulated our ethos — a hug, a touch that broke months of isolation. Rooted in the conviction that every individual, regardless of their circumstances, deserved care steeped in dignity and compassion, our founders pioneered innovative approaches to palliative care. Casey House emerged not just as Ontario's first free-standing hospice, but as a trailblazer in end-of-life care and HIV/AIDS health services, all within an environment that mirrored a home's comforting embrace.

Amidst the challenges, this era was also characterized by a surge in activism and heightened awareness. Many organizations were established in the late 1980s to support people living with HIV and AIDS, and many individuals cared for friends and family. A leader amidst this movement was June Callwood, who aptly noted, "We are taking care of people in ways they can accept." This sentiment continues to resonate within the very essence of Casey House, where care embodies a deep understanding of the human experience. In acknowledging June's legacy, we pay tribute to the countless individuals who have ardently contributed to nurturing the flame of compassion that continues to illuminate the corridors of Casey House.

Reflecting on the past thirty-five years necessitates an acknowledgment of the initial years of the AIDS crisis — a period marked by profound loss and the heartbreaking disintegration of a community. Gay men were decimated by the disease, and the survivors, the family and friends of those who died, grappled not only with the death of a singular friend or partner but with a cascade of losses. The enduring trauma born from those challenging times remains palpable, etched into the minds of those who bore witness to the tragedy of the era. Dr. Gregory Robinson, who lives with HIV, describes this time: "Funerals, visitations, and memorials were always part of our weekly schedule. A few people with AIDS and HIV infection were overwhelmed with fear and desperate for release and found their only option was suicide. Some went to the grave without even being known to have suffered with AIDS. Parents and siblings of those affected were at times absent due to homophobia and AIDS stigma. Year after year we continued to bury our friends...our community. Casey House has always been a beaming light in our darkest days."

Fortunately, since then significant strides have been made in the treatment of HIV, and receiving a diagnosis no longer carries the weight of a death sentence. With widespread access to testing and treatment, life expectancy for individuals with HIV is now aligned with the average age in Canada. The landscape has transformed, with mortality rates experiencing a dramatic decrease when comprehensive testing and therapeutic options are accessible..

Regrettably, despite the progress made in HIV treatment, many continue to experience significant systemic barriers to health care. These barriers continue to highlight the pressing need to ensure equitable access to health care services for all. Dismantling these barriers remains a crucial step in creating a health care system that serves all Canadians.

Consequently, Casey House's commitment endures, transitioning from its initial role as a hospice to that of a specialized hospital. This evolution reflects an ongoing dedication to adapt and expand services, ensuring that the organization can effectively meet the evolving needs of those affected by HIV.

Embracing a commitment to inclusivity, Casey House expanded its reach in 2021 beyond its initial focus, recognizing the imperative to extend care to those who continue to experience systemic barriers to health care. This progression includes a shift from solely catering to individuals with a positive HIV diagnosis to welcoming clients who are part of communities experiencing higher rates of HIV due to the social and structural determinants of health. This includes individuals facing poverty, homelessness, unstable housing, substance use and mental health challenges, as well as those who have been incarcerated. Notably, our inclusivity extends to trans folks and MSM (men who have sex with men). This transformation is deeply rooted in the lessons taught by the LGBTQ2S+ community, enriching Casey House's DNA with the wisdom of creating a haven for those who need it most.

We continue to be a beacon of warmth and acceptance, providing health care that is not just compassionate but free from judgment — a place where compassion and social justice meets care provision.

On behalf of our community, we extend our deepest gratitude to Nick Green and everyone involved in bringing Casey House's story to life. We are touched and honoured to be singled out as the backdrop for Nick Green's important telling of queer Canadian history. Thank you for striving to centre the humanity of people living with HIV in this narrative. Through this play, we hope to not only honour the past but inspire a future where compassion knows no bounds.

Joanne Simons
CEO, Casey House
Fall 2023

Production History

Casey and Diana was originally commissioned by the Stratford Festival, Ontario, Canada, through the Foerster Bernstein New Play Development Program. The première production opened on June 1, 2023, at the Stratford Festival Studio Theatre. Antoni Cimolino, Artistic Director, and Anita Gaffney, Executive Director.

Cast:

Thomas:	Sean Arbuckle
Pauline:	Laura Condlln
Marjorie:	Linda Kash
Andre:	Davinder Malhi
Diana:	Krystin Pellerin
Vera:	Sophia Walker

Creative Team:

Director:	Andrew Kushnir
Dramaturge:	Bob White
Designer:	Joshua Quinlan
Lighting Designer:	Louise Guinand
Composer and Sound Designer:	Debashis Sinha
Supervising Fight Director:	Geoff Scovell

Stage Manager:	Michael Hart
Assistant Stage Manager:	Sam Hale

Apprentice Stage Manager:.............Cassie Westbrook

Production Stage Manager:.................... Michael Hart

Production Assistant: ....Emma Jo Conlin

Technical Director:...............................Tristan Goethel

Assistant Director: ....Damon Bradley Jang

Assistant Set Designer: .... Katriona Dunn

Assistant Costume Designer:......... Barbara Morrone-
Sanchez

Assistant Lighting Designer...... Aidan Jackson-Hoag

Producer:..David Auster

Casting Director:..Beth Russell

Creative Planning Director:...................... Jason Miller

Director of New Plays:............................ Keith Barker

Sean Arbuckle as Thomas and Krystin Pellerin as Diana, Stratford Festival, 2023. Directed by Andrew Kushnir. Designed by Joshua Quinlan. Lighting designed by Louise Guinand. Photo by Cylla Von Tiedemann. Photo courtesy of the Stratford Festival.

Characters

Setting

The play takes place at Casey House in the week leading up to Princess Diana's visit on October 25, 1991. There are several playing spaces on the stage, with the main one being the bedroom. While this one is adorned in a more literal way, as described below, the other spaces can be represented either literally or conceptually. Lighting will be an important aspect of defining these spaces, which include a nurse's station, a lounge with a telephone in it, a bench outside, and a church. There is also a space with the corner window of Casey House and June's desk, where the lit candle is displayed when someone passes away.

The bedroom, which should be central, is a double resident's room. At Casey House, the beds were not side by side as the rooms were often irregularly shaped. The room also has a couple of chairs, some tables/counter space, and room for personal belongings. There is a window next to Thomas' bed.

Act One

Scene 1 – Your Highness

> *Lights up on THOMAS, VERA, and DIANA. They are in his room. THOMAS is lying on his bed, looking at DIANA. DIANA is standing across the room. VERA stands by the bed.*

VERA: Your Highness, I would like to formally introduce you to Thomas.

THOMAS: *(Laughs.)* I'm really nervous.

DIANA: So am I.

VERA: Should I leave you then, or would you like me to—?

THOMAS: Could you find my sister?

VERA: I'll look for her.

THOMAS: Good.

> *THOMAS raises his hand towards DIANA, expectantly. There's a pause.*

THOMAS: Oh, I'm sorry. That was too forward. I was told you touch people.

VERA: I'm sure it was okay. There's just protocol, so—

DIANA crosses the room and takes THOMAS' hand.

DIANA: Thank you.

VERA: Alright.

VERA exits. There is a pause.

THOMAS: Here we are at last.

DIANA: At last.

THOMAS: I know it's stupid to start with, but I want you to know that I watched every single minute of your wedding. My sister and I, she stayed the night and we watched the whole thing together in the morning, which is a big deal because we had to get up at something around five a.m. to catch it over here and she does not do mornings. We watched from the start of that carriage ride. I kept thinking what could possibly be going through her mind? On the one hand, there were thousands of people there to see you. On the other, that ride must have felt like forever. I was wondering; were you just totally drinking the moment in? Or were you wishing those freaking horses would trot a little faster so you can get there and get on with it already? I can't imagine wishing that ride away, but I also can't imagine the anticipation.

When you arrive at the church, these two girls in matching white dresses are waiting for you on the long red carpet that stretches up the stairs. The carriage pulls up and the door opens and you emerge, looking like this giant ball of Kleenex. I mean, a really beautiful ball of Kleenex, of course. Your dress stretches out behind you; going on, and on, and on. The girls in white appear by your side to help manage your train, so careful, almost as if afraid to touch you. Then, kind of like you suddenly realize that people are watching, you turn and look out. A huge cheer thunders through the air as you raise an arm. You giggle, and for a second the veil slips and we see a twenty-year-old who thinks this is all just as nuts as the rest of us. And then you turn to your father. There's a second of comfort within this unbelievably surreal moment. Then, back in action. Trumpets blare as you take the rest of the stairs, head up, eyes set on the destination.

My sister and I talked about how unbelievable it would feel. I said that I think my head would've exploded. How can anyone be in a moment of such wild fantasy and still be alive?

But your head didn't explode... apparently. People don't die in situations like this. They take a breath and proceed, which is what you did. You take your father's arm, and.... Whoosh. You walk nervously and fiercely into your new life and your train stretches on and on; a beautiful slip of yourself holding on to the world behind, leaving a mark that you were there, a remnant of your beauty and innocence sliding gracefully and blowing softly in the wind.

> THOMAS smiles. DIANA takes hold of his hand.

When I go, I want my ghost to have a train. Is that too much to ask?

DIANA: Not at all.

THOMAS: Beggars can't be choosers, I guess. I mean I
                got to make it to today, so I already owe one to
                the almighty whoever. I swear there are claw
                marks in the hardwood. One more week, we
                screamed, clinging like cats to a screen door.
                One more week! Your Highness, let me tell
                you, it was a very long week.

Scene 2 – New Roommate
October 17, 1991

> *We are brought back to the day that ANDRE arrived at Casey House — October 17, 1991. ANDRE enters in a wheelchair, pushed by VERA. MARJORIE follows.*

ANDRE: This isn't... No. This is wrong. No.

THOMAS: *(To DIANA.)* It was the longest week of our lives.

> *DIANA exits as ANDRE continues into the room.*

ANDRE: *(Head in hands.)* Listen, I can't stay here.

VERA: Marjorie, could you get Andre some water?

> *MARJORIE crosses to get water and glass.*

ANDRE: I don't want water.

THOMAS: Who do we have here?

MARJORIE: New roommate.

THOMAS: Well, yippee skippy.

VERA: Do you want to get into bed or stay in your chair for a bit?

ANDRE: I want to go home.

> *MARJORIE crosses to ANDRE with the water.*

THOMAS: Try clicking your heels together.

ANDRE: *(To MARJORIE.)* I'm not thirsty!

MARJORIE: Sorry.

THOMAS: Excuse me, did anyone catch the reference?

VERA:	The paramedic said you were having some pain. Can I give you something for that?
ANDRE:	No.
MARJORIE:	I'm a volunteer here, by the way. Marjorie. I can stay with you for a while if you'd like. Help you get set up or keep you company…?
ANDRE:	Shut up… *(ANDRE groans and turns away.)*
THOMAS:	*(Whispers.)* I think he likes you.
MARJORIE:	Should I do the intake form?
ANDRE:	No more forms.
VERA:	You can do it tomorrow.
THOMAS:	Well, I don't know how you'll fit it into the social calendar. We've got cocktails on the lanai, followed by shuffleboard on the aft deck, then, of course, aerobics at—
ANDRE:	The guy at the hospital said I'd get my own room.
VERA:	This is what we had available. Thomas is a great roommate.
THOMAS:	*(Laughs cynically, then with Southern accent:)* "Don't try to get on my good side Truvy, I no longer have one."

THOMAS smiles at ANDRE, expectantly.

ANDRE:	What?
THOMAS:	*Steel Magnolias. (Beat.)* You… haven't seen it?
VERA:	Oh boy.
THOMAS:	Well it's a medical emergency…
ANDRE:	This is bullshit. It's not fair.

THOMAS: Amen.

VERA: What can I get you?

ANDRE: My own room!

VERA: Take a few deep breaths.

THOMAS: Don't worry, I should be moving any day now.

              Beat.

VERA: It's late. Why don't you see how you feel in the morning?

              ANDRE nods.

VERA: Marjorie, can you help me with the bed?

              MARJORIE crosses to ANDRE's bed.

THOMAS: You, darling, are my fourth roommate in five months. Been here the longest of anyone. (Golden Girls *quote, as Blanche:*) "Amazing that I can feel so bad and look so good."

MARJORIE: What's that, Murphy Brown?

THOMAS: Murphy Brow— how dare you. So there's me, then the next longest is Leonard, then— *(As VERA assists ANDRE out of his chair.)* leave some room for Jesus, Vera. Leonard, then Vince, then Ken....then what's-his-name... he has the most attached earlobes I've ever seen...

MARJORIE: His name is Corey.

THOMAS: Hm. So you've noticed it too.

VERA: Why don't you get up for a walk or something?

THOMAS:	Are you trying to get rid of me?
VERA:	Yes. And you've been lying there for two weeks. You'll keep getting those sores.
MARJORIE:	*(Refilling ANDRE's water cup.)* There's water right here if you need it, and you can call for a nurse any time. *(She puts the water on his side table.)* You okay?
ANDRE:	Am I okay?
MARJORIE:	I just meant—
ANDRE:	Am I okay? *(He tears up.)* Am I okay?

ANDRE rolls in bed, back to her. Beat.

THOMAS:	I think that's a no.
VERA:	You should get some rest. Call if you need anything. *(To THOMAS.)* You be nice.
THOMAS:	I'm a pussycat.
MARJORIE:	Sleep tight.
THOMAS:	Bye.
VERA:	Want the lights out?
THOMAS:	Please.

VERA and MARJORIE exit. ANDRE and THOMAS have a quiet moment.

THOMAS:	Thank God *they're* gone.

No answer. ANDRE adjusts, reaches down and massages his shins and feet.

THOMAS:	Neuropathy?

ANDRE glances at him, then looks away.

THOMAS: Epsom salts and a warm bath, I've seen it work wonders.

ANDRE lies back down and turns his back.

THOMAS: How old are you?

No answer. ANDRE turns off the light.

THOMAS: Okay. Good night.

Scene 3 – For Jacob
That night

> *VERA and MARJORIE enter a hallway downstairs. MARJORIE heads towards JUNE's desk.*

MARJORIE: Sorry, I'm such an idiot. *Are you okay?* Should I go back and apologize?

VERA: We all do it. Honestly. Don't punish yourself.

MARJORIE: Thomas was in a mood tonight.

VERA: You should've seen him yesterday. I'm hoping having a roommate again will help.

MARJORIE: I don't know how you do this job. Are you married?

VERA: No.

MARJORIE: Going home to an empty house after this...

VERA: I have a girlfriend.

MARJORIE: Oh. That must help.

VERA: Sometimes.

> *MARJORIE sets to work: she gets a fresh candle out of a box, takes the old candle off the stand on JUNE's desk, puts the new one on.*

VERA: Who's the candle for?

MARJORIE: Jacob.

VERA: We lit one for him two days ago.

MARJORIE: We actually didn't. It was already burning for Morris, and then we kept it lit for Curt, so then this afternoon should have started for Jacob, but the candle burned out.

VERA: Oh. You are way past the end of your shift.

MARJORIE: It takes a minute.

VERA: *(Beat.)* No, sure. Yeah.

MARJORIE: *(Gestures to the candle.)* I know you were close to—

VERA: No, you go ahead.

MARJORIE picks up the matches, strikes one, and lights the candle.

MARJORIE: For Jacob.

VERA: For Jacob.

A beat as they reflect. VERA closes her eyes and takes a deep breath.

MARJORIE: It's too bad he isn't around for the big visit.

VERA opens her eyes and looks around, ensuring no one heard, shushing MARJORIE.

MARJORIE: Everyone's in bed.

VERA: Still.

MARJORIE: *(Quietly.)* I feel like he would have loved it.

VERA: *(Laughs.)* He would have screamed.

MARJORIE: I can't wait to see everyone's faces. When are you telling them?

VERA: Jane wants us to spread the news first thing tomorrow.

MARJORIE: It's so exciting!

VERA: Yes, it will be. We have to get there first.

MARJORIE: It's on the 25th. She's coming in a week!

VERA: No, Marjorie. She's coming in seven days.

Lights shift. They exit.

Scene 4 – Frankie's and Diana
The next morning: October 18, 1991

> *The bedroom. THOMAS and ANDRE are in their beds. ANDRE is sleeping.*

THOMAS: Marco.

> *No answer.*

THOMAS: Marco.

> *ANDRE stirs slightly, opens his eyes.*

THOMAS: Marco!

ANDRE: *(Sits up in bed, startled.)* Jesus. What?

THOMAS: You're supposed to say Polo.

ANDRE: You woke me up.

THOMAS: Just making sure you're still here. *(Beat.)* You were awake, I saw you. It's nine, they're doing rounds soon.

ANDRE: *(Rolling over, burying his head in his pillow.)* They can just wake me up when they get here.

THOMAS: Sure, if you'd rather be roused by the calloused hands of a certain resident nurse, suit yourself.

> *MARJORIE enters abruptly.*

MARJORIE: Marco!

THOMAS: Polo!

> *ANDRE lets out a frustrated groan.*

MARJORIE: Oh no, sorry. I woke you.

THOMAS: Oh please, he's fine.

MARJORIE:	Some people like to sleep in.
THOMAS:	I've never been able to sleep in. Way too many years doing the brunch shift. *(To ANDRE.)* You ever go to Frankie's Diner? Maybe I served you.
ANDRE:	No.
THOMAS:	What?!
MARJORIE:	*(Over THOMAS, above.)* Really?! Gay breakfast!
THOMAS:	Gay breakfast! Worst food you've ever tasted. I mean we're talking barely edible.
MARJORIE:	I have hair on my chest from that coffee.
THOMAS:	Well and also menopause. Come on, every homo's been to Frankie's. Not once?
ANDRE:	No.
THOMAS:	Wow. Kids these days. No appreciation for tradition.
ANDRE:	Maybe we don't want shitty eggs.
MARJORIE:	*(Laughs.)* Touché.
THOMAS:	That was not a touché.
ANDRE:	I need to use the phone.
MARJORIE:	We were supposed to do this intake form last night.
ANDRE:	You were supposed to let me use the phone last night.
THOMAS:	*Touché.*
ANDRE:	Five minutes.

MARJORIE: Okay.

VERA enters as MARJORIE is helping ANDRE into his chair.

VERA: Good morning. Oh. What's going on here?

ANDRE: I'm using the phone.

VERA: Okay, I'll come back to you two.

MARJORIE: Oh, is it time to— you're going to—?

VERA: Yes.

MARJORIE: *(To ANDRE.)* You should stay, you'll want to hear this.

THOMAS: What?

VERA: I can come back.

MARJORIE: No, no. *(To ANDRE.)* Trust me.

THOMAS: What the hell are you talking about?

VERA: Well… okay, thanks Marjorie. I've been, umm… I was asked to speak with all the residents this morning about a piece of news that's, well… kind of interesting.

MARJORIE chuckles, reacting to this extreme understatement.

We are going to have a visitor coming and doing a tour. Someone who will likely, um, draw quite a bit of media attention…

THOMAS: Who is it?—

VERA: Well… it's, um… Princess Diana.

Beat. THOMAS' jaw slowly drops.

MARJORIE: Isn't that exciting?

ANDRE: We get to meet her?

VERA: She's going to go room by room and will meet everyone who's here. There will be about a million rules to follow and a ton of preparation, so it should be quite interesting... and... exciting.

THOMAS: You're lying.

MARJORIE: It's true.

THOMAS: Vera, I swear to Madonna Louise Ciccone if you're making this up—

VERA: *(Laughs.)* I'm not making it up. She's coming.

THOMAS: I... uh. I don't... Princess...?

MARJORIE: Princess. Diana!

THOMAS: Princess Diana. *(He looks to ANDRE, who's smiling. He laughs.)* There's a smile, Andre. Princess freaking Diana— That'll make any homo smile. Oh my God. When is she coming?

VERA: In... seven days.

ANDRE: Holy shit.

THOMAS: ...Seven days. Holy shit. Seven days...

MARJORIE: Exciting news, isn't it?

ANDRE: Yeah, it's... yeah.

                     Beat.

VERA: You can go use the phone now.

                     ANDRE and MARJORIE exit.

VERA: I need to check your back.

THOMAS: Mhm.

> *VERA crosses to THOMAS.*

VERA: Breathe.

THOMAS: I am breathing.

> *She undoes the back of his gown and lays her hand on his shoulders.*

THOMAS: Ow!

VERA: I barely touched you.

THOMAS: Are you part sandpaper?

VERA: Can you get on your side?

> *He shifts and lies still for a moment as VERA works.*

THOMAS: I hadn't planned on being here next week.

VERA: I know.

THOMAS: Well thanks for the pep talk.

VERA: Just breathe.

> *Beat.*

THOMAS: Princess Diana.

VERA: We'll take it day after day.

THOMAS: Yeah sure. *(Beat.)* Oh God stop staring at me. *(Golden Girls:)* "You have Bette Davis eyes and Freddy Krueger hands, Blanche."

VERA: Thanks. Take your meds. I'll be back in a bit.

> *VERA exits as DIANA enters.*

THOMAS: *(To DIANA.)* Seven days. Really?

Scene 5 – Rent
Later that day

> *MARJORIE and ANDRE are at the nursing station. At the top of the scene, ANDRE hangs up the phone, having finished his call.*

ANDRE: Shit!

MARJORIE: No answer?

ANDRE: No.

MARJORIE: Do you want to try calling someone else?

ANDRE: I don't know.

MARJORIE: If you have an address book, I can go and get it.

ANDRE: Like what am I supposed to do?

MARJORIE: Who are you trying to call?

ANDRE: No one.

MARJORIE: You know, I could help you. That's kind of what I'm here for.

ANDRE: I don't need help, I just need him to answer the phone.

> *He picks up the phone and dials again. He waits while it rings, then sighs and hangs up. He puts his face in his hands.*

MARJORIE: Maybe try again later. Don't let it spoil the happy news.

ANDRE: Do I have to talk to you?

MARJORIE: You don't have to do anything.

ANDRE: Okay, bye.

MARJORIE: I'm sorry, correction; you have to have some manners, please.

ANDRE: What?

MARJORIE: You don't have to speak to me, but when you do, you don't speak to me like that. Okay?

ANDRE: Okay.

MARJORIE: Great.

                        Beat. ANDRE sighs.

ANDRE: No one knows I'm here and I don't want my landlord to call my mom.

MARJORIE: Why would he?

ANDRE: Couldn't he get the number through the bank or something? When he doesn't get my rent?

MARJORIE: I don't think so.

ANDRE: I'd rather he just throw everything out.

MARJORIE: Why don't you call a friend?

ANDRE: I don't have anyone's number.

MARJORIE: I can get the phone book.

ANDRE: I only moved here like just less than a year ago, so...

MARJORIE: Oh. *(Checking the coast is clear.)* Well, I could go by and get some of your things, if you want.

ANDRE: Are you allowed?

MARJORIE: I've only been here a month. I could plead ignorance.

ANDRE:	You'd do that? Because I need more clothes. And some books. And my Walkman.
MARJORIE:	Sure. I'll even hide the dirty magazines.
ANDRE:	What? No.
MARJORIE:	Make a list and give me your keys.
ANDRE:	You don't want to go there. It's a room in a house and it's a total shithole and the landlord's super creepy—
MARJORIE:	Andre. Let me take care of you. I've been doing this a long time.
ANDRE:	You've been here a month.
MARJORIE:	Oh, honey. I've been doing this since before you were born.
ANDRE:	You really don't have to—
MARJORIE:	I won't pass judgment about your shithole, I swear.
ANDRE:	Okay.
MARJORIE:	Perfect. Now can we do this goddamn intake form or what?
ANDRE:	I'll think about it.

MARJORIE exits with ANDRE.

Scene 6 – Tiny Simple Things

> *DIANA is sitting by THOMAS' bed as before.*

THOMAS: I thought no way, seven days no way! A couple more days, max. Maybe if I'm lucky I can get close enough that they can tie me to Vera and sort-of *Weekend at Bernie's* me through the whole thing.

DIANA: Well, that's a morbid image.

THOMAS: God knows I'm more than halfway there.

DIANA: You look wonderful.

THOMAS: Please. I look like a member of the road company of *Cocoon*. Sorry. *Golden Girls* reference. My stupid, awful sister would have gotten that but no one else.

DIANA: Stupid and awful sister? I don't like the sound of that.

THOMAS: Well, she wasn't always stupid and awful. She was my everything for most of my life. Took me to my first ever gay bar, actually. Talked every day, part of all my friend groups. Pauline. Then I got sick and told her and she was gone. The old predictable.

DIANA: People are scared of the illness, not the person.

THOMAS: Still makes them assholes. Anyways, so they told me you were coming, and I was lying there trying not to disintegrate into a pile of mixed emotions, and then I started thinking about that dress of yours...

DIANA: You're going to need to be a little more specific.

THOMAS:	The one you wore to your engagement party. Black, strapless taffeta by… um—
DIANA:	The Emanuels. I love that dress. I thought it was beautiful and perfect. That sentiment wasn't completely shared, of course. But it's just a silly dress, we have much more important things to talk about.
THOMAS:	Are you KIDDING??! This is like the homosexual version of the Make-A-Wish Foundation.
DIANA:	Well, listen. The moment I was seen by… *(Raises eyebrows.)* … it was *You're not wearing that, are you?* Hours I spent, deciding, only to be met with *You're not wearing that, are you?* Do you know what I did?
THOMAS:	You wore it.
DIANA:	I wore it. And I looked positively stunning, I don't mind saying. I paired it with a huge smile all night long. It felt torturous while I was doing it, hearing people talk about how black is for mourning and how inappropriate it was and what a terrible message I was sending about my taste. But I wore it well.
THOMAS:	Perfectly. And this is what I was thinking about. Overnight, something as simple as getting dressed…
DIANA:	You have no idea. Before, I never spent more than an hour getting ready. I hardly thought of it, beyond what looks halfway pretty. Then suddenly, it was what I wore, my hair, how I sat, what I ate, every little thing became consuming.
THOMAS:	So then what did you do?

DIANA: Well, I guess I thought that if all the tiny simple things like picking out clothes are going to become so incredibly hard, then I simply need to become incredibly good at them.

THOMAS: Exactly. All the tiny simple things you never thought of before. I was thinking about you and all the huge changes and challenges and how you got through. All the tiny little things. *(Beat.)* After Vera left, I saw you across the room in my mind's eye. You were there sitting in the chair. I saw you and at first I thought…seven days. No way. And then I thought…okay, how about one minute? All the tiny simple things. Heart beating, none of my business; breathing, yep, that'll happen on its own. Swallow, blink, stretch my neck a little, alright, that was easy, I got that down, and then about twenty seconds of toe wiggling. Whoosh, one minute down, feeling good. And there you were.

DIANA: Shall I…?

THOMAS: That would be lovely.

DIANA crosses to the chair.

THOMAS: So I'm picturing you there and I thought… okay, how about one minute more? Blink, stretch the neck, and then move the hands a little. Flatten the palms then bend the elbows, and push? No, need to flex the abs a bit, and that one's not so fun but do it quickly and then push and nudgey-wiggle your way up and up and up and then… *(Sighs.)* I'm sitting up. Whoosh, one more minute down and I'm already sitting up. And I imagined you saying something like *You can make it.*

DIANA: You can make it.

THOMAS: I'm frankly a little exhausted and my back is
                screaming, but you're repeating that.

DIANA: You can make it.

THOMAS: Exactly. And I think okay, one more minute,
                tiny simple things, blink, neck, hands, abs...
                and legs? Legs. *(He slowly, painfully swings
                his legs over the edge of the bed.)* Legs... legs...
                legs... legs... Legs. And... *(He puts his feet on
                the ground.)* feet. Ahhh. You can't imagine
                the feeling of putting your bare feet on the
                ground after being in bed for two weeks. It's
                a kind of cool that ripples into your whole
                body. It makes your breath catch. And then...
                whoosh, one more minute I'm standing and
                you're smiling and I'm thinking there must
                be more gas in the tank than I thought. Maybe
                I could... maybe I could... *(Very slowly at
                first, building momentum.)* Maybe I could hip.
                Thigh. Knee. Fall forward. Heel ankle foot.
                Shift. Hip. Thigh. Knee... every step a little fall
                heel ankle foot. Shift. Fall, heel, foot, fall, heel,
                foot. The mechanics of the ankle. The angle of
                the heel coming in contact with the ground,
                and then the spreading of the foot. All the
                tiny things. One more minute, two minutes,
                closer. I could see myself getting closer and
                closer. Closer and closer! Closer and closer to
                you...!

                *Lights shift. DIANA remains. THOMAS
                walks around the room, then crosses to the
                doorway.*

THOMAS: *(Yelling out the door.)* Attention! Attention,
                everyone! May I have your attention please?!
                Rafael, Vince, Ken! Listen up, Andre! I have

an announcement! I have decided that WE ARE GOING TO MAKE IT! We are going to sit up in bed, and eat, and do our hair... if applicable. Get dressed—oh my God, what to wear?! Jerome? Leonard? Some sign of life, please? Seven days of life, then go when you want. But seven days—!

VERA enters the room and tries to escort THOMAS to bed.

VERA: What are you doing?

THOMAS: *(Resisting at first.)* Promise me. Blood brother promise! Come on!

VERA: Let's go, back to bed.

THOMAS lets her lead him away.

THOMAS: Okay, okay. Day after day! Put on your Sunday best! Practise your curtsies! *(He breaks away, back to the door.)* WE'RE GOING TO MEET A PRINCESS!

Lights shift. VERA leads THOMAS back to bed as he speaks to DIANA.

THOMAS: I swear, I absolutely swear that hope has a sound.

DIANA: It's a faint, warm ringing in your ears, isn't it?

THOMAS: Exactly. That day as I walked through the house, in my ears. That night as I tried to sleep, through the walls and floors. The next morning, the whole house. A faint, warm ringing. Hope. The whole house was ringing.

The phone rings at the nursing station. Lights shift.

Scene 7 – Chopping Carrots
The next morning: October 19, 1991

> *The nursing station. MARJORIE enters.*
> *She answers the phone.*

MARJORIE: Good morning... No, it's Marjorie, but I can find her if you'd like. Oh, okay... I don't know, I've only just arrived for the day... Well, it's rather early so I'm not sure if he's awake yet, but I can check if you'd like... Yes, but he may be sleeping. Who's calling please? Oh, okay... bye.

> *She hangs up the phone. VERA enters.*

VERA: Good morning. You're back.

MARJORIE: Yes. It's Saturday.

VERA: You've been here a lot this week.

MARJORIE: Big visit coming. *All hands.* I've talked about it with Ruth.

VERA: Good. They're short in the kitchen today.

MARJORIE: Oh, trust me, they don't want me in there.

VERA: I can relate, but anyone can chop carrots.

MARJORIE: Alright. *(Beat.)* Quite the speech Thomas made yesterday.

VERA: Yeah.

MARJORIE: Everyone's so excited.

VERA: I know. Which is great...

MARJORIE: What?

VERA: No, it's great.

MARJORIE:	Didn't you hear Thomas? They're all going to make it!
VERA:	I don't want anyone to be disappointed.
MARJORIE:	Well, they won't be disappointed, Vera. They'll be dead. Excited, then dead.

Beat.

VERA:	I know that..

MARJORIE begins to exit.

VERA:	Where are you going?
MARJORIE:	I wanted to pop in on Andre.
VERA:	He's fine. I'll be seeing him in a minute for rounds.
MARJORIE:	I'm just saying hello.
VERA:	Might be better to do it later. Or your next shift.
MARJORIE:	I'm just saying hello. Dear.
VERA:	Okay.
MARJORIE:	And then I'll report for duty in the kitchen.
VERA:	Thank you.

MARJORIE exits, leaving VERA to her work.

Scene 8 – Sweater
The same morning

> *In the bedroom, early. THOMAS rolls over in bed.*

THOMAS: Marco.

> *ANDRE sighs.*

THOMAS: I know you're awake. Marco.

ANDRE: Polo.

THOMAS: Was that so hard? How'd you sleep?

ANDRE: I kept waking up with no idea where I was.

THOMAS: Sounds like me in my twenties.

ANDRE: You were talking to yourself all night.

THOMAS: To myself? Or was I awake and talking to you?

ANDRE: I think you were dreaming.

THOMAS: Have you heard of sundowning?

ANDRE: Yes.

THOMAS: Sometimes at night… it hasn't happened in a while…

ANDRE: I think you were dreaming.

THOMAS: Yeah. Probably. Well... I'm off. *(Starts to get up.)* Morning constitutional. I thought I'd hit Queen's Park for a bit of love, then head down to the steps, maybe some dancing…

ANDRE: Have you actually cruised in Queen's Park?

THOMAS: Of course, who hasn't?

A quiet beat.

THOMAS: You haven't missed much. Deep shame and grass stains mostly, which are both, of course, simply impossible to get rid of.

THOMAS takes his walker and makes his way out of the room. MARJORIE enters carrying a duffel bag.

MARJORIE: Good morning, everyone.

THOMAS: Oh wow, look at that big bag.

MARJORIE: Yeah, it's something I got for— ... you meant me, didn't you.

THOMAS: Yes, I did.

THOMAS exits. MARJORIE glances out the door to check the coast is clear.

MARJORIE: We have to act fast. I got your stuff.

ANDRE: Already?

MARJORIE: I'm a morning person. Listen, if Vera asks—

ANDRE: I'll say my landlord sent it over.

She opens the bag and lays stuff out.

MARJORIE: Perfect. The books. I couldn't find the Sue Grafton, thankfully, but I got the others. Your cassette player and a bunch of tapes. I can't believe you like the Sex Pistols.

ANDRE: I like lots of old music.

MARJORIE: *(Beat.)* Well that one hit me right in the gut. *(Passing tapes and Walkman to him.)* Now, for clothes, I only had the one bag, so I'll have to make another trip.

ANDRE: Did you bring my varsity jacket?

MARJORIE: I, uh, no. I mostly grabbed sweaters and cozies.

ANDRE: Which sweaters?

MARJORIE: These two casual ones, both very nice.

ANDRE: Aaah, I was hoping you'd get that one.

                MARJORIE tosses it to him, then pulls out a nice new sweater.

MARJORIE: I also found this, maybe for the visit.

ANDRE: I haven't worn that one yet.

MARJORIE: I was going to say it looks brand-new.

ANDRE: Yeah. *(Beat.)* I bought it months ago to wear out in the village, or… I don't know...

MARJORIE: Try it on.

                She tosses him the sweater.

ANDRE: Why?

MARJORIE: Because I want to see.

ANDRE: I'm tired.

MARJORIE: Do it. Come on. Good. Do you want me to help you?

                He puts it on, slowly noticing that the sweater is very large on him.

ANDRE: No.

MARJORIE: Fix the collar. It's a very nice sweater. Sit up, Andre, let me see.

ANDRE:	Fine.

He sits up. He looks down, realizing.

MARJORIE:	Charles is going to have some competition. *(Beat.)* You look great.

Beat.

ANDRE:	Great? This used to fucking fit me.

ANDRE takes the sweater off and drops it on the floor.

MARJORIE:	I could have it taken in for you.
ANDRE:	No. Thanks.
MARJORIE:	Sorry.

ANDRE sinks back into bed. Beat. MARJORIE crosses back to the bed. She sees something in it and has an idea.)

MARJORIE:	*(In a cutesy voice:)* Let me out! I want to see my fwiend! *(In her voice:)* Oh, you want to come out now, do you? *(Cutesy voice:)* Pwease Mawjowie pwease wet me owt. *(Her voice:)* Okay, come on out…

She reaches into the bag and pulls out a stuffed bear and brings it over to him.

MARJORIE:	*(Baby voice:)* Hewwwo Andweeeyyyy!
ANDRE:	Oh my God.

He grabs it and pulls it under the covers.

MARJORIE:	What's his name?
ANDRE:	Carl.

MARJORIE: So you're into bears, are you? *(She laughs at her own joke while ANDRE blushes.)* I also brought you a journal. I'd actually bought it for Thomas, but he told me that the only people who write in journals are lesbians and psychopaths. Do you want it? *(Puts it with his things.)* I have to get to kitchen duty. Make another list and I'll go back, but be specific this time.

ANDRE: Thank you.

MARJORIE: You're welcome. Oh, and Andre... I found your dirty magazines.

ANDRE: You did?

MARJORIE: *(As she exits.)* No. But now I know you have some.

Lights shift.

Scene 9 – Lionel Richie
October 20, 1991

THOMAS enters with DIANA.

THOMAS:	Oh, the fresh air! I started by walking the length of the hallway, then down to the front door. By the next day I was up and down the street, and then around the block.
DIANA:	Out in the fresh air.
THOMAS:	Yes. Heaven. Pure heaven. *(Beat.)* Okay, I'm just going to ask. How is this going so far?
DIANA:	What? Our visit?
THOMAS:	I hope you're not plotting your escape.
DIANA:	Well, it's hard to run in heels.
THOMAS:	I spent days preparing so that I wouldn't break etiquette, and then as soon as you walked in it all right down the shi— ...out the window.
DIANA:	You're doing perfectly.
THOMAS:	Oh, come on, I'm a mess! I addressed you before you addressed me, which is…
DIANA:	*(Gasps dramatically and clutches her pearls, then quickly shifts.)* I really couldn't give a damn.
THOMAS:	I knew it! They made it all sound so serious.
DIANA:	Well, it's not to me.
THOMAS:	And what about *His* Highness...?
DIANA:	Oh, he cares.
THOMAS:	Ah.

DIANA:	Oh yes, he really cares. His Royal Highness.
THOMAS:	Right. *I knew that!*
DIANA:	It's all so strange. One minute I'm out in a crown, people curtsying and calling me by title, and the next I'm on the sofa with crisps watching *Beverly Hills 90210*.
THOMAS:	I don't even know where to begin with that piece of information.
DIANA:	We're all people, aren't we?
THOMAS:	We are. So then how would you like to be greeted?
DIANA:	How about… Hello, Diana.
THOMAS:	Oh, I couldn't.
DIANA:	Of course you can.
THOMAS:	It feels wrong, I don't know, it makes me wiggly.
DIANA:	It's perfectly natural. You're Thomas, I'm Diana. Hello, Thomas.
THOMAS:	Hello…. No. No no.

THOMAS turns away, she touches his arm.

DIANA:	Wait, stay here. Hello, Thomas.
THOMAS:	I'm going to have a stroke.
DIANA:	You're fine. Perfectly natural.
THOMAS:	Perfectly… perfectly perfect.
DIANA:	Hello, Thomas.
THOMAS:	Hello—

PAULINE enters.

PAULINE: Tommy. Hi.

                    THOMAS turns and sees PAULINE. Beat. He looks back at DIANA.

THOMAS: And of course she had to show up and ruin everything.

Scene 10 – Walks Like a Duck

> *THOMAS crosses downstage with PAULINE following him.*

THOMAS: I said go away, Pauline.

PAULINE: Just talk to me for a second.

THOMAS: How dare you come here?!

PAULINE: Tommy.

THOMAS: Don't call me that.

PAULINE: Your name?

THOMAS: Only dead people call me that now.

PAULINE: But that's what I call you.

THOMAS: And you're dead to me.

PAULINE: How can you say that?

THOMAS: *(Southern accent, quoting* Steel Magnolias:*)* "I'm not as sweet as I used to be."

PAULINE: I'm sorry, okay? I wasn't thinking. I was angry.

THOMAS: I'm not doing this.

PAULINE: My therapist thinks that I—

THOMAS: Therapist!? *(A cruel laugh.)* You just throw that in there all nonchalant — *my* therapist.

PAULINE: I've been seeing a therapist. He's really helped—

THOMAS: Oh my God. Yes, of course you're seeing a therapist. That's exactly what you would do. Psychologize yourself into believing that *you're* the victim.

PAULINE:	That is not true!
THOMAS:	And then show up here to—to break everything again!
PAULINE:	Nothing's broken.
THOMAS:	EVERYTHING is broken! You abandoned me!!
PAULINE:	You played a part in this, too, and you know it.
THOMAS:	What?
PAULINE:	The names you called me.
THOMAS:	Walks like a duck.
PAULINE:	Tommy.
THOMAS:	Thomas. I'm dying with my full name. It's a matter of integrity.
PAULINE:	Just talk to me for a second.
THOMAS:	How did you even know I was here?
PAULINE:	I've been calling, and I—
THOMAS:	Oh my God.
PAULINE:	What?
THOMAS:	You heard.
PAULINE:	What do you mean?
THOMAS:	About who was coming to visit.
PAULINE:	Well, I read about it, but no, that's not why—
THOMAS:	You thought that you'd get a chance to meet her.
PAULINE:	No. What? No!

THOMAS: I can't freaking believe you.

PAULINE: I didn't even know you were in a HOSPICE, TOMMY!

THOMAS: WHERE ELSE WOULD I BE?!

PAULINE: I came here to see you.

THOMAS: Yeah? Then how about a hug? No?

PAULINE: That is not fair.

THOMAS: Come on. It's Tommy!! You asshole. You disappointment. Why would you come here?! You were dealt with, Pauline! You were gone!

PAULINE: No, I wasn't!

THOMAS: *(Face in hands.)* What have you done?

                    VERA enters.

VERA: Everything okay?

PAULINE: I don't think he's feeling well.

THOMAS: It's broken again.

VERA: Need to go back to your room?

THOMAS: Yes.

PAULINE: I'll be back, Tommy. I'll be here again tomorrow.

THOMAS: With any luck I won't be.

                    THOMAS exits with VERA behind, helping.

PAULINE: Excuse me, I'm his sister, Pauline—

VERA: Hi—

PAULINE: Can you tell me how he's doing?

VERA: *(Catching up to THOMAS.)* Sorry.

                 *VERA exits. PAULINE stands for a
                 moment.*

PAULINE: I'll be back, Tommy!

                 She hesitates, then exits.

Scene 11 – What Is That Smell?

> *In the bedroom, ANDRE is in bed reading. MARJORIE enters like a secret agent holding a large brown paper bag.*

MARJORIE: *(Conspiratorially.)* The dog barks at midnight, but only when the moon is full.

ANDRE: Um. Are you okay?

MARJORIE: I come bearing top secret contraband.

ANDRE: What?

MARJORIE: You are sworn to secrecy.

ANDRE: Is it... weed?

MARJORIE: Weed?! No. You think I'd bring you dope? *(Holds up takeout bag.)* You think I'd bring you this much dope?!

ANDRE: What did you bring?

MARJORIE: You won't tell anyone?

ANDRE: I won't.

MARJORIE: Alright. *(She removes a container from a paper bag.)* One order coming up.

> *She puts it down in front of him. He opens it.*

ANDRE: Eggs?

MARJORIE: From Frankie's Diner.

ANDRE: I thought they were disgusting.

MARJORIE: It's a rite of passage.

ANDRE:	You brought me breakfast.
MARJORIE:	I brought you gay breakfast!
ANDRE:	Why is this so top secret? We're allowed outside food.
MARJORIE:	Not when it's one step from poison. I got some for Thomas, too, and I was hoping he might even sort of serve it, for fun.
ANDRE:	It smells like—
MARJORIE:	Cat food.

MARJORIE pulls a chair next to the bed, starts sorting out the different containers and pulling out cutlery.

MARJORIE:	Let's eat while it's still somewhat warm.
ANDRE:	You're eating too?
MARJORIE:	We are in this together, honey. *(MARJORIE is setting up and dishing food out as she speaks.)* It was a real trip walking into Frankie's. I used to be there at least a few times a month when Michael was around. First time I've been in there since he died. It was… very strange.

MARJORIE pauses as a wave of emotion comes over her.

ANDRE:	Who's Michael?
MARJORIE:	Best friend of thirty years. *(Composing herself.)* Sorry. We were teachers together. I taught English and I was mostly a good teacher but never great. Michael taught music and the kids loved him so much.
ANDRE:	When did he die?

MARJORIE: Seven months ago. I cared for him at home until the end. Almost. He had kids from a previous marriage, they hated me, hardly let me see him. Blah blah. So listen, here's the lay of the land at Frankie's: when you walk in, there's a booth by the window, and a line of booths down the left-hand side. I want you to picture it, it's all a part of the experience. There's this big "Wait To Be Seated" sign, and Andre, you wait to be seated or you have Lorna to deal with, which is... strangely thrilling... So you're seated and Thomas or another server comes along and is sure to point out how haggard you look. Coffee comes right away, and usually you just order the eggs. You don't think about it, your order is just business, it's not the point. You are seated in a one-stop shop of best friends and ex-lovers. You are surrounded by hundreds of flimsy pictures of legends and strangers that are pinned to the walls. You are completely unable to hear your friend when someone still in drag gets Lorna to blast Whitney Houston while straddling an eighty-year-old lesbian at the bar. All the while, because you're as handsome as Michael, you're pretending not to notice a guy two booths down who's staring like you're a scoop of ice cream on a summer day. It's muggy in there, it's packed and you're breathing everyone into your body with every single breath. And then the cat food eggs arrive, and you dig right in. *(She gestures at his plate.)* Dig in.

ANDRE: Okay.

MARJORIE: *(Raises her fork.)* God bless. Penance for a life of only the best kind of sin.

　　　　　　ANDRE takes a bite.

ANDRE:	It's not that bad.
MARJORIE:	I actually rather like it, but don't tell anyone. *(She takes a bite, then in a queeny manner:)* Oh bitch, these are disgusting.
ANDRE:	*(Catching on.)* Sweetie, they're egg-trocious.
MARJORIE:	*(Laughs.)* Egg-zactly! Gay breakfast!

Another bite. Beat.

ANDRE:	Saturday breakfast was a big deal with my family. I mean it probably still is, I don't know.

As ANDRE goes to take a bite—

MARJORIE:	—Don't eat the potatoes. *(Beat.)* When did you stop having breakfast with them?
ANDRE:	Years ago, when they stopped inviting me, even though I lived in their basement. I was working nights at this gas station, though, so I didn't really care. And that was obviously before they kicked me out.
MARJORIE:	Why did they kick you out?
ANDRE:	Honestly, it's so boring.
MARJORIE:	I'm not bored.
ANDRE:	I am. What's the next topic?
MARJORIE:	Oh, I don't know… men?
ANDRE:	Ugh. I hate men.
MARJORIE:	Me too, darling, me too.

THOMAS enters, irate.

THOMAS:	What is that smell?!

MARJORIE: Oh, Thomas! You're here.

ANDRE: Guess what Marjorie brought.

THOMAS: No.

                He steadies himself against the bed.

MARJORIE: I brought some for you.

ANDRE: You'll like it.

THOMAS: Ugh, it's making me nauseous.

MARJORIE: Sounds about right. I'll serve him.

                *ANDRE passes her the package with eggs.
                She balances it on her hand and crosses to
                him.*

MARJORIE: Here you are, sir, order's up—

                *THOMAS lashes out, angrily, knocking
                the carton out of her hand.*

THOMAS: I don't want it!

ANDRE: Hey—!

THOMAS: Get it out of here, it's making me want to
                throw up!

                *MARJORIE hastily starts to clean up the
                mess, as well as the other cartons of food.*

ANDRE: She was doing something nice.

THOMAS: Yeah? What's in it for her?

ANDRE: Nothing. Why are you being an asshole?

THOMAS: I AM an asshole. Everyone's an asshole,
                damn it!

                VERA enters.

VERA:	You okay, Thomas?
THOMAS:	Did she leave?
VERA:	She left.

THOMAS paces, unsteady.

THOMAS:	I can't believe… Now?!
VERA:	Why don't you sit down?
THOMAS:	How did she even find me? Did someone tell her?!
VERA:	No! We don't give out that info.
THOMAS:	Well she figured it out, didn't she?! Why did she have to— *(Moans. He stumbles, VERA steadies him.)* The past, the past… what is that smell?!
VERA:	*(Guiding him to the bed.)* Lie down.
THOMAS:	It was behind. I had closed it. There was a plan!
VERA:	You need to rest.
THOMAS:	It's gone, it's all… BACK!!
MARJORIE:	Do you want some water?
THOMAS:	No.
VERA:	Rest.
THOMAS:	I just want to… What's the…? *(He crumbles.)* It's ruined!!

THOMAS starts to cry. Long beat. VERA puts her hand on his shoulder and looks to the others, who are watching silently, unsure what to say.

VERA: I'm so sorry. *(Beat.)* Do you need anything?

THOMAS, head in pillow, begins muttering to himself.

Thomas? Marjorie, can you close the curtains and turn on the lights, please? Do you want a snack? *(Beat. She waits for a response, there is none.)* How about some company? Marjorie can sit with you, or I can stay for a bit.

THOMAS brushes her away. The muttering has stopped.

Alright. How about some space. Try to rest, but try not to nap, okay?

VERA squeezes his shoulder, then goes towards the door, then hesitates—she's never seen THOMAS like this. She gestures to MARJORIE.

VERA: We'll come back in a bit, okay?

MARJORIE moves in to THOMAS, gently and encouraging.

MARJORIE: You know... we're only five days from the big visit. Everyone's doing really well. I think that speech you made really helped.

She gestures to VERA to confirm.

VERA: Yes, definitely.

No response from THOMAS.

MARJORIE: Five days, she'll be walking in the door, probably hundreds of people outside, and she'll be walking into this room here. Get to chat a bit. You're going to need to be prepared. Have you figured out what you're going to say, Andre?

ANDRE:	No.
MARJORIE:	Really? You haven't figured it out?
ANDRE:	I have no idea.
MARJORIE:	Well, I bet Thomas can help you out. He probably knows exactly how this goes. Right, Thomas? Have you figured out what you're going to say? *(Beat. THOMAS doesn't answer.)* No? Well you guys need to be prepared! She'll be sitting right here in just a few days! You could ask about *Buckingham Palace* and Prince Charles. I bet they'll even take a picture—
THOMAS:	No.
MARJORIE:	What?
THOMAS:	*(Steely.)* No, Marjorie. No. That is not how it goes. Buckingham Palace, a picture. That is not how it goes. Okay?
VERA:	Okay.
MARJORIE:	Okay.
THOMAS:	This. *This* is how it goes. There are hundreds of people outside and she pulls up in a car to see *ME* and NOT Pauline. *(Rising up in bed.)* She gets a tour around the house and is led up the stairs to meet ME, AND NOT HER. She comes in this room, looks around, and locks eyes with ME, and NO ONE is taking that. It's mine! It's my moment, I'm holding it. And *this* is how it goes. This is how it goes:

She locks eyes with me, and everyone else in the room, in the house disappears. Everyone in our lives disappears because the moment we see each other, we will both know that we've been waiting all of our lives to meet and that the day has finally come. I am *not* going until that day, alright?

And when I go it won't be just another *Oh did you hear about Thomas, another one for the tally, another drop of water in the tidal wave, sad smile he'll be missed bullshit* BULLSHIT! Me off floating in the whatever, thinking *what the hell was the point of that*?! It'll be *Did you hear about Thomas ushered off this earth by a* PRINCESS, oh well, isn't that poetic, doesn't that make sense. Because it ALL makes sense this way. And it'll be MINE. Not painful, Pauline. Not yours. And I'll tell her thank you. I'll say *Your Highness, thank you for giving me this moment. Thank you for reminding the world that we matter, and that no one is above compassion.* And she'll hold my hand and smile.

    Beat.

MARJORIE: That was good. *(To ANDRE.)* You should just steal that.

    Beat. THOMAS looks over at MARJORIE, shocked. Another beat. He laughs.

THOMAS: Yeah, right. When she gets to Andre, he's going to be so star-struck and unprepared, he'll just lie there and kind of gape like a fish on the deck of a boat.

ANDRE: She'll come to me before you probably, and I'll remember everything you just said.

THOMAS: It'll be hard to talk with a pillow held over your face.

VERA: Easy, now.

THOMAS: Wait! Wait, I forgot my favourite part. I almost forgot the ice-breaking question I'm going to start with. Because you have to break the ice.

MARJORIE: Right.

THOMAS: *Your Highness, what are you going to be for Halloween next week?* It seems stupid, but I have a feeling that someone as sharp as she is will have the most perfect, brilliant, genius answer that will bond us instantly. Princess Diana, what will you be for Halloween? And she'll say....come on, think about it... something really scary... and she'll say...?

ANDRE: What?

VERA: *(Gets it.)* A queen!

THOMAS: Exactly! A queen! A queen!

Lights shift.

Scene 12 – Chrissy Turlington
October 20 to 22, 1991

> *Lights change to isolate characters in different positions on stage. DIANA enters, standing by THOMAS. He talks to her.*

THOMAS: Five days left. Your Highness. The ringing returned. It was almost able to drown out everything else. Do you know what I mean?

DIANA: I do.

THOMAS: Bathed in that sound, we all sat up a little further in bed.

VERA: Vince is feeling better today.

MARJORIE: Corey wants to get dressed.

THOMAS: We ate a few more bites of dinner—

ANDRE: Can you help me into my chair?

MARJORIE: Of course.

THOMAS: Got outside.

VERA: Leonard was wondering if he could join you on a walk.

MARJORIE: Two more bites of eggs.

THOMAS: Every morning, that ringing grew a little louder.

> *PAULINE enters.*

PAULINE: Thomas.

THOMAS: Princess!

ANDRE: Diana!

THOMAS:	And no one died. Over those days, as we all sat up, so did the staff.
VERA:	There are more requests for shaving.
MARJORIE:	I'm an excellent barber.
THOMAS:	You're not getting near my face again.
MARJORIE:	That was one time!
THOMAS:	We could see, in the space of a couple days, a change.
ANDRE:	Are we allowed to put posters on the wall?
VERA:	Let's open some windows.
THOMAS:	We had gone from dying to trying to stay alive. And no one died.
VERA:	We're only four days out.
PAULINE:	Thomas.
MARJORIE:	I brought that blanket you wanted.
ANDRE:	My mom made it.
THOMAS:	That ringing got louder, and we sat higher.
VERA:	She's here again.
THOMAS:	No.
MARJORIE:	Should we get outside?
PAULINE:	Thomas, please talk to me.
ANDRE:	What are you doing today?
THOMAS:	Sat a little higher, walked a little further.
PAULINE:	Thomas.

THOMAS: Got outside.

ANDRE: Can I come?

MARJORIE: Only three more days.

THOMAS: Ringing louder, so close!

MARJORIE: So close.

VERA: So close.

THOMAS: We're going to make it!

PAULINE: Tommy!

ANDRE: So close.

THOMAS: We're going to make it!

            Lights out on all but THOMAS.

THOMAS: Please! Let us make it.

            Lights snap out.

            End of Act One.

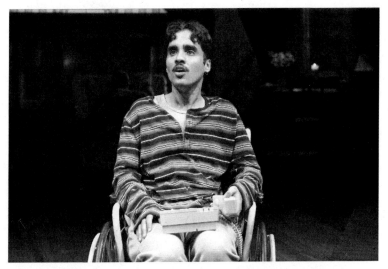

Davinder Malhi as Andre, Stratford Festival, 2023. Directed by Andrew Kushnir. Designed by Joshua Quinlan. Lighting designed by Louise Guinand. Photo by Cylla Von Tiedemann. Photo courtesy of the Stratford Festival.

Sophia Walker as Vera, Stratford Festival, 2023. Directed by Andrew Kushnir. Designed by Joshua Quinlan. Lighting designed by Louise Guinand. Photo by Cylla Von Tiedemann. Photo courtesy of the Stratford Festival.

Linda Kash as Marjorie, Stratford Festival, 2023. Directed by Andrew Kushnir. Designed by Joshua Quinlan. Lighting designed by Louise Guinand. Photo by Cylla Von Tiedemann. Photo courtesy of the Stratford Festival.

From left: Laura Condlln as Pauline, Linda Kash as Marjorie, Davinder Malhi as Andre, Sean Arbuckle as Thomas, Sophia Walker as Vera and Krystin Pellerin as Diana, Stratford Festival 2023. Directed by Andrew Kushnir. Designed by Joshua Quinlan. Lighting designed by Louise Guinand. Photo by Cylla Von Tiedemann. Photo courtesy of the Stratford Festival.

Act Two

Scene 1 – Gay Polar Bear
October 22, 1991

> *THOMAS and ANDRE are in bed. It's morning. THOMAS sits up.*

THOMAS: Marco.

> *Beat, no response.*

THOMAS: Marco.

> *A beat, still no response.*

THOMAS: Oh God, are you in a mood again? Marco.... *(Pause. THOMAS sits up in bed.)* Andre? *(He swings his legs over, nervous.)* ...Andre?

> *Beat, then suddenly, with a quick middle finger:*

ANDRE: Polo!!

> *THOMAS shrieks.*

THOMAS: Oh my sweet mother Dolly PARTON WHAT THE HELL?!?!

> *ANDRE laughs, very pleased with himself.*

THOMAS: NO! NOT FUNNY! You could have killed me! I am very delicate!

Beat. They both get the giggles.

THOMAS: Pretending to be dead. That's dark.

ANDRE: Shut up, let me sleep.

THOMAS: You finally have the Casey House humour. You only get it when you're in the club.

ANDRE: Lucky us.

THOMAS: Did you hear the one about the gay polar bear—?

ANDRE: Oh my God, go back to sleep.

THOMAS: You have to laugh to keep from dying.

ANDRE: Okay then, tell me a million jokes.

THOMAS: Knock, knock.

ANDRE: Who's there?

THOMAS: Screaming warthog.

ANDRE: Screaming warthog who?

MARJORIE enters.

MARJORIE: Good morning!

Beat.

THOMAS: I swear I did not know she was coming.

MARJORIE: What?

MARJORIE is carrying shaving supplies, including a basin of water, towels, and a bag of equipment. She sets it all down.

THOMAS: I was just about to head out on my walk, and Andre was going to join me in his chair.

ANDRE: No, I wasn't. *(To MARJORIE.)* Can you open the window?

> *THOMAS gets out of bed and starts getting ready; putting on a sweater, shoes.*

THOMAS: Oh, come on, I'll push you the whole time this time.

ANDRE: I'm too tired.

MARJORIE: Did you have a rough night?

ANDRE: Um, yeah.

THOMAS: Why?

ANDRE: I couldn't really sleep and then I kept thinking about my mom, and how—

THOMAS: Why couldn't you sleep? Was I acting weird?

ANDRE: Kind of...

THOMAS: I was? Weird how?

ANDRE: You kept telling me to go out and buy you a Popsicle.

THOMAS: Oh my God, Popsicles. I'm always going on about Popsicles.

ANDRE: You were, uh, kind of giving me the eyes. And you called me... Sugar Lips..

THOMAS: Oh really. *(Bursts out laughing.)* Well, don't you worry, I was sundowning, I guess. Huh. Stupid sister set me back a week. All the more reason to get walking. Come onnnnnn, Andre, don't make me go alone.

MARJORIE: He's getting a shave.

THOMAS: *(To ANDRE.)* What, from The Demon Barber of Huntley Street?

MARJORIE: Hey! I'm very good at it.

THOMAS: Sure. Last shave you'll ever need.

MARJORIE: *(Laughs)* Oh stop.

THOMAS: *(To ANDRE, as he exits.)* I'm brunching with Ken, so you have an hour to change your mind. Good luck with Sweeney Toad.

MARJORIE: *(Laughs.)* Yeah?! Well, good luck with... Sweeney... JERK! *(Beat as MARJORIE accepts that it simply was not funny, she mutters:)* Forget it.

Scene 2 – A Nice Shave

> *She turns back to ANDRE.*

MARJORIE: Did you sleep at all?

ANDRE: Maybe an hour.

MARJORIE: You must be exhausted.

ANDRE: Is that going to happen to me? Sundowning?

MARJORIE: I—um… No, I doubt it.

ANDRE: He didn't know who I was. It was still him in his eyes, but he was somewhere else.

> *MARJORIE sits on the edge of his bed.*

MARJORIE: He's okay now.

ANDRE: Yeah. Did you open the window?

MARJORIE: I did, but the air's not moving. So listen, I went to the drugstore to buy you an actual razor because the ones here—

ANDRE: I think I want to call my mom.

MARJORIE: Oh.

ANDRE: I can't stop thinking about it.

MARJORIE: The things you told me about her—

ANDRE: It's my mom.

MARJORIE: Yeah, yes, obviously.

ANDRE: There was this cycle in my head last night when Thomas would sleep for a bit. This ringing, and then *Hello? Ma? It's me.* And her *Hello?* And this ringing….Am I making sense?

MARJORIE:	Yes.
ANDRE:	I was thinking, if I called her and we talked things out, she could get all my stuff out of the apartment.
MARJORIE:	Well, lots of it is here in storage.
ANDRE:	But then what about… after I… after?
MARJORIE:	Don't let *logistics* be the reason you call.
ANDRE:	I know. But also… Princess Diana. She loves her. I mean, if she knew she was coming…
MARJORIE:	Okay. Sure—
ANDRE:	Will you do it with me?
MARJORIE:	If you decide you want to.
ANDRE:	I think I should. Now.
MARJORIE:	Now?
ANDRE:	Yes.
MARJORIE:	Andre, it might not go well.
ANDRE:	Someone should know… I know, should… *(He sighs, tired.)* Someone I know should know where I am. Right?
MARJORIE:	I know where you are, and that's good for this morning. Why don't you just relax for a bit, okay? You're exhausted. Nice little shave, head back, relax okay?

> *ANDRE settles back, and MARJORIE sets to work shaving his face. Lights shift.*

Scene 3 – Policy
Same day.

> *PAULINE strides onstage, VERA following.*

VERA: Excuse me, I told you to stop.

> *PAULINE stops, turns around.*

PAULINE: You can't force me out of here.

VERA: You're on private property.

PAULINE: Have you even checked? Have you even told him about the two times I came yesterday?

VERA: Yes.

PAULINE: You don't understand what you're doing.

VERA: I do, actually. Do you?

PAULINE: What is that supposed to mean? I'm trying to see my brother. My brother.

VERA: I'm sorry, but he doesn't want to see you.

PAULINE: You can't talk to me like that.

VERA: That's where it starts and stops with our policy.

PAULINE: *(Approaching VERA.)* Oh my God, your policy. Is that your favourite word? Policy? Is it your policy to alienate people from their family?

VERA: Okay, I'm calling the police.

PAULINE: Oh, come on. Ridiculous!

VERA: You have entered a private area without permission—

PAULINE:	Call them!
VERA:	—and you are getting into my personal space.
PAULINE:	They'll probably arrest you for the inhumanity of it all.
VERA:	Alright. *(She starts to head off.)*
PAULINE:	Wait. *(Beat.)* Don't call the stupid police.
VERA:	You have one minute to leave.
PAULINE:	What, do you have a stopwatch?

VERA glares at her, expectantly.

PAULINE:	Okay, okay!

She starts to exit.

PAULINE:	I get carried away. It's a family trait. *(She stops.)* I'm desperate. Sorry.
VERA:	I understand.
PAULINE:	Is it pointless? I told my boss I have the flu. I should have said mono. Do you think I should stop coming? You probably *can't* answer that. Sorry. I, uh… I don't want to lose him. I actually wrote a few things down. *(She starts looking through her purse.)* I have this therapist… you don't care. I thought that I could read this out if… —Actually… could you give this to him?

She pulls some folded-up papers from her purse. It's a letter.

VERA:	I can ask if he wants it.
PAULINE:	Yeah, but make sure he looks at it. Please.
VERA:	I'll bring it to his room.

PAULINE: Where should I—

> *VERA holds out her hand. PAULINE puts the letter carefully into her hand.*

PAULINE: Don't read it. Do you have any tape?

VERA: No.

PAULINE: Okay. Thank you.

VERA: Sure.

PAULINE: I'm uh... I'm not going to come back again unless he calls me. Uh... Can you tell him that?

VERA: I'll tell him.

PAULINE: Thank you.

> *PAULINE exits. VERA puts the letter in her pocket and exits opposite. Lights shift.*

Scene 4 – Come On
Same day

> *MARJORIE is sitting next to ANDRE's bed, reading. ANDRE is sleeping. THOMAS enters.*

THOMAS: *(Holding up a newspaper.)* We're in the news again!

MARJORIE: We are?

THOMAS: Vince just showed me. Corey was being all cynical and boring about it, but Vince and I were losing our minds. Listen: *(Reads.) All over Ontario today, last-minute details are being furiously shoehorned into place to ready the province for its visit later this week from that most stellar of royal couples.*

MARJORIE: Mmm, I get called that all the time, too — most stellar.

THOMAS: I think you mean "Old Yeller." *(Reads.) Organizers are quick to caution that one must not read too much into the separateness of the agendas. They are being portrayed as a modern-day working couple.*

MARJORIE: Oh yes, he with his job in the coal mines, and she with her paper route.

THOMAS: You done? *(Reads.) Charles will deal largely with the —*

> *VERA enters.*

VERA: Good morning.

> *THOMAS groans, annoyed about being interrupted.*

VERA: Is he sleeping?

MARJORIE:	Yes, he was up all night.
THOMAS:	Oh, that was my fault. Apparently, I triggered a sexual awakening.
VERA:	I have his medications. Yours, too.
	She hands THOMAS his pills; he takes them.
MARJORIE:	You can leave Andre's, I'll give them to him when he wakes up.
VERA:	I'll come back. *(To THOMAS.)* Your sister was here again.
THOMAS:	Oh, for God's sake.
VERA:	She asked me to give you this.
	She holds out the papers.
THOMAS:	Burn it.
MARJORIE:	What is it?
VERA:	I'm just going to leave it here, and you can decide what you want to do with it.
THOMAS:	Fine. Got a light?
MARJORIE:	Aren't you curious?
THOMAS:	I'm sure it's intolerable and filled with bad grammar.
VERA:	Maybe take a look.
THOMAS:	Et tu, Boobus?
VERA:	It's up to you, obviously—
THOMAS:	Yu-huh.

VERA: But she's not coming back unless she hears from you, so this could be it.

THOMAS: Great. Hallelujah. I'm busy. *(Picks up the newspaper and finds his place.)*

MARJORIE: We're in the paper.

VERA: Ah.

THOMAS: Here it is: *Casey House, Canada's only free-standing hospice for people with AIDS, is hoping for a boost of publicity from Diana's efforts.*

MARJORIE: That's it?

THOMAS: Yes. But. They mentioned us last which means we're clearly her favourite. It's obvious.

VERA: That's exactly what I was thinking.

THOMAS: Alright, well, you two stay here and work on your feigned enthusiasm. I'm going for a walk with Ken. *(THOMAS gets his coat and a hat, pauses.)* How long ago did she leave?

VERA: About ten minutes. Towards Yonge.

THOMAS: Okay. You're sure?

VERA: I'm sure.

MARJORIE: Maybe you should wear a disguise, just in case.

THOMAS: Oh, good idea. Can I borrow your mustache?

MARJORIE: Brilliant. No one would recognize you with hair.

THOMAS: That was good.

          ANDRE suddenly writhes in bed, letting out a cry of pain.

MARJORIE:	Andre?
	VERA goes to his bed. He is doubled over on his side.
MARJORIE:	What's wrong?
VERA:	Andre? Andre, can you hear me?
	ANDRE starts to shiver, he moans.
MARJORIE:	What's happening?
VERA:	*(With forced calm.)* Go get the doctor.
MARJORIE:	He was fine, he was just sitting up!
VERA:	Marjorie, go get the doctor...
	MARJORIE leans over ANDRE.
MARJORIE:	Andre? You're okay. *(To VERA.)* Do something! DO SOMETHING! You're okay, you're okay...
THOMAS:	Marjorie, give them some space.
MARJORIE:	Andre! Andre, wake up!
VERA:	Calm down.
MARJORIE:	Calm down?
VERA:	Or step outside until you can—
MARJORIE:	What are you talking about?!
VERA:	Step outside.
MARJORIE:	No. *(She takes ANDRE's hand.)* Andre? You're alright, wake up. Wake up, Andre—
	VERA heads to the door.

Where are you—? Why didn't you give him his pills?! You should have given them to him. Why didn't you—?!

VERA gives MARJORIE a hard look, then exits. MARJORIE leans over his bed. ANDRE has gone still.

MARJORIE: Don't leave! Andre? No, come on. No, you didn't—you didn't... No, come on come on come on come on. Andre, come on... come on. Come on... Andre. *(She paces, then goes back to his bed.)* Wake up, I'm here. Andre, here I am, come on. Andre? Come on. COME ON!!

Beat.

THOMAS: Shit.

Lights switch, MARJORIE hanging on to ANDRE, THOMAS looking on.

Scene 5 – The Door Opens
That evening

> *DIANA enters, THOMAS speaks to her in the room. MARJORIE remains with ANDRE.*

THOMAS: People can get used to anything, you know what I mean?

DIANA: I'm not sure that's right.

THOMAS: No?

DIANA: People can numb to anything.

THOMAS: Very true. Roommate number four. An infection that came on fast. At first he was out and in, but when he was in he was practically out. And then he was just out. Marjorie sat next to his bed all day, all night and into the next morning, crying and whispering.

DIANA: It's so unbelievably sad.

THOMAS: It is, it is. But yet I... ate lunch, read for a bit, ate dinner. I sat and looked out the window. Marjorie's sniffs and crying, the underscoring of my life. I stared at the street and I felt numb.

Andre moved in the day before they told us you were coming. He'd been in the hospital and they drove him over in an ambulance. It's not far, but the ride would have felt like forever. He was in the back and can see out the rear windows, driving to the place he's going to die. Do you think he was wishing away his last minutes in the world so he could just get there already? It's so unbelievably sad.

I can see out my window here when he pulls up on the street. The back doors open, and Andre is lowered out in a wheelchair by these two paramedics, all in white, practically hazmat suits. Gloves, masks, gowns, hardly touching, like they're afraid to breathe. Andre looks out at the neighbourhood where people stop, watching him. Suddenly Vera appears at the door; she's seen all this happen through the window. She walks out, crouches down, and wraps Andre in this huge hug right there in the middle of the street. A second of comfort in a surreal moment.

She turns him towards the door and he looks up, almost seeing me in my window. He's a young, skinny kid looking at the place where he's eventually going to die. And it's so, so, so sad. Why doesn't his head explode? Why didn't mine? How can anyone face down this incredible nightmare and still be alive? A moment that every gay guy I know has imagined and thought *What if that is me one day?*

But people's heads don't explode. They take a breath and proceed, and so does Andre. Whoosh. He moves forward, brain detached from body, towards his new life. And death. He reaches the door, takes a breath and it is incredibly, incredibly sad. He goes in, and the door closes, and his old life is gone. Everything is gone.

The door closes and the whole world is gone. You take a breath and the door closes and gone, gone. That's right isn't it? Gone.

MARJORIE: *(Quietly, to ANDRE.)* Please don't go, Andre. Please please please.

THOMAS: But then…

               THOMAS looks at her, struck by her pain. He sees PAULINE's letter on the bed. He picks it up and reads it. As he does, PAULINE enters and sits on a bench downstage. THOMAS folds the letter back up and thinks.

THOMAS: The door closes, and your world is gone. So quickly, so quickly. But everyone else…

               PAULINE turns and sees THOMAS. She stands and gives a meek wave.

PAULINE: Thomas.

               He hesitates.

PAULINE: Hi.

               THOMAS gets out of bed. He walks downstage to where PAULINE is sitting.

THOMAS: The next afternoon…

               Lights shift.

Scene 6 – Shitting Fuck
October 23, 1991

> *Our Lady of Lourdes church. THOMAS sits on the bench, keeping a distance between them.*

PAULINE: I could have met you at the house.

THOMAS: I needed to get out of there.

PAULINE: But I mean… a church?

THOMAS: It was a trap. I thought you'd burst into flames.

> *PAULINE lets out a loud laugh.*

THOMAS: Shh.

> *Beat.*

PAULINE: Thank you for calling me. *(Beat. She waits for THOMAS to speak, but he's still formulating his thoughts.)* I thought I'd be late. I had to come all the way in from Scarborough. *(Beat.)* I live there now. I got a basement suite. Closer to work.

> *THOMAS pulls out PAULINE's letter, tosses it on the pew.*

THOMAS: What is this?

PAULINE: My Hail Mary pass? That's a sports reference.

THOMAS: No joking.

PAULINE: Okay.

> *THOMAS opens the letter.*

THOMAS: *(Reads mockingly:) When you told me that you were sick, I felt angry because I was going to lose you. When you said that you have AIDS, I felt scared because Jamal had just died. When you called me a bitch, I felt —*

PAULINE: Yeah, yeah, I know what it says.

THOMAS: What is this?!

PAULINE: It's, um, well, it's called non-violent communication.

THOMAS: It's called garbage.

PAULINE: Then why are you here?

THOMAS: Closure.

PAULINE: I don't believe you.

THOMAS: I'm here to tell you to move on. You don't need to visit or write embarrassing essays or apologize anymore. You don't need to cry next to my bed. You're free.

PAULINE: You don't get to decide that.

THOMAS: You abandoned me.

PAULINE: And I'm trying to explain!

THOMAS: With this? This is the most violent communication.

PAULINE: Fine, sure. I'm pure evil. Everything is my fault! Shit, is that closure?!

THOMAS: *(Sharply hushing her.)* You don't swear in here.

PAULINE: *(Hushed.)* Well fu—... Tommy the things you said. I deserve an apology too. The names—

THOMAS: That was in reaction to what you did.

PAULINE:	So beyond that.
THOMAS:	Please, you've been called way worse..
PAULINE:	Never.
THOMAS:	Right.
PAULINE:	You said that I'm worse than Mom and Dad.
THOMAS:	Well.

Beat.

PAULINE:	Still? You haven't thought that one out? You don't want to take that one back?
THOMAS:	You disappeared on everyone. The minute someone got sick.
PAULINE:	That's not true.
THOMAS:	Sitting at the back of their funerals doesn't count.
PAULINE:	I was doing my best.
THOMAS:	That's what I was saying at first, she's doing her best. Then it kept happening, another one sick and you can't make it out for drinks. Then I'm only seeing you when it's us. Then I got sick, and told you... The look on your face, the flinch. Mom and Dad all over again.
PAULINE:	Don't you dare say that one more time.
THOMAS:	You wouldn't even touch me. Move on, Pauline. Please.

Beat. THOMAS turns to leave.

PAULINE:	No. Don't leave. Tommy. *(Yelling, her voice echoing in the church:)* Shit! Damn it! Shit! Shit!!

> *THOMAS turns back to her, urgently shushing—*

THOMAS: Stop swearing!

PAULINE: Do you know, um—Tommy, when you told me—!

THOMAS: I don't care.

> *He goes to leave again.*

PAULINE: Fuck! Shit fuck!

THOMAS: *You're in a goddamn church.*

PAULINE: I'm going to fucking keep shit bitch swearing....

THOMAS: Stop it!

PAULINE: Then shitting listen to me, fuck.

THOMAS: What? Say it then!

PAULINE: I, uh. Okay. Uh. *(Beat.)* Do you remember, at all those funerals—when I would sit at the back apparently, even though that's not true—do you remember the dress I always wore? The one with the big shoulders? My funeral dress. So I found it the other day when I was doing a clean-out because my awful apartment only has one closet—

THOMAS: Poor you. Bye.

PAULINE: Neil... Your friend Neil died, and I felt just close enough to come with you to the funeral. I threw on the dress and came out to get you to zip it up and you gave me this look and *You're not wearing that, are you?* Thank you so much. You thought the shoulders were too big, but I wore it anyways and I looked great.

Next thing I knew, you were zipping me up in that dress once a month, then twice a month, then once a week. That dress went from paying respects to acquaintances to saying goodbye to my closest friends. I went to Richard's funeral in a dress he had complimented the week before. Jason asked me to pair it with a veil for his to which I said *Oh, we're taking requests now*, and then about three weeks later I had to ask myself whether or not he was joking. Do you know, Thomas, do you know that I couldn't wear that dress to Jamal's funeral because it was at the dry cleaners? Think about that. I didn't have time to get my funeral dress cleaned between funerals.

Tommy. Tommy. I'm sorry. I freaked out. You tried to hug me, and I flinched and backed up. That was so shitty, it was a shitty, disgusting reflex, but it's scary, okay? Everyone is dying!! That scares me. I was handling it, I was keeping my paranoia and stupidity at bay, but then you... we're basically one person, so if it can get you... and it is not rational but it's effing terrifying, so there. And maybe that makes me an awful, ignorant person, but worse than Mom and Dad? I spent most of my life protecting you from Dad, and I mean come on, Mom? I didn't go to college so that you could live with me... Worse than them? So I ran away. I'd been so barely holding it together in the first place, Tommy. And it's not an excuse, it's not about making excuses, it's just the truth. I avoided you for a while, and then it became a long while, and then I didn't know what to say to you and I was so MAD at you. And then I assumed you wouldn't want to hear from me and then I was too ashamed to try and make things right. And then I found that black dress and nearly gagged on *my own effing tears* because I realized that I'd way rather wear the dress than have no one left to wear it for.

You've always said that the only person who's a bigger asshole than you is me, and if you don't freaking forgive me, I'm about to prove you more right than you ever thought possible. Please, Tommy. I forgive you. Please.

> *Long pause. THOMAS looks at her, then looks away. He sits back down on the pew, then looks at her.*

THOMAS: What are you doing with your hair?

PAULINE: It's a perm.

THOMAS: You look like a llama.

> *They both laugh.*

PAULINE: *(Steel Magnolias:)* "Laughter through tears is my favourite emotion."

> *Beat.*

THOMAS: You're not like Mom and Dad.

PAULINE: I know!

THOMAS: I never should've said that.

PAULINE: Thank you.

THOMAS: But you need to build a bridge and get over your bull-dookie. I mean it.

PAULINE: I know I know I know. I'm working on it.

THOMAS:	With your *therapist*.
PAULINE:	Fuck off.

They laugh. Beat.

THOMAS:	Throw out that dress. Black is so overdone.
PAULINE:	Maybe a nice floral?
THOMAS:	*(Steel Magnolias:)* "My colours are blush and bashful."
PAULINE:	*(Steel Magnolias:)* "Your colours are pink and pink."
THOMAS:	I really missed you.

Lights switch.

Scene 7 – The Tour
Same day

> *MARJORIE sits by ANDRE's bed, playing solitaire. VERA enters. She pauses at the door when she sees MARJORIE. MARJORIE gives her a frosty look.*

MARJORIE: I'm here as a visitor.

VERA: I know.

> *VERA crosses into the room and does some checks on ANDRE.*

VERA: Have you been home?

MARJORIE: I went home this morning, took a shower.

VERA: How long do you plan on staying?

MARJORIE: I haven't set an agenda.

> *Beat.*

People get upset.

VERA: They definitely do.

MARJORIE: And yet you felt the need to go to Ruth about me—

VERA: Yes.

MARJORIE: —and say I'm "too attached—"? What is that supposed to—?

VERA: Marjorie, if you're here as a visitor, then be a visitor.

MARJORIE: What do you have against me?

VERA: We can have a meeting with Ruth next week—

MARJORIE: People get upset. It's a human thing that humans do.

VERA: I know that. I am one, too.

> *VERA begins to exit, then stops next to the door.*

Can I ask you a question?

MARJORIE: Okay.

VERA: Why do you want to volunteer here?

MARJORIE: Excuse me?

VERA: Why do you want to volunteer here?

> *MARJORIE scoffs and looks away.*

VERA: You've lost a friend to AIDS. Is that right?

MARJORIE: I've lost a lot of friends.

VERA: Recently.

MARJORIE: I know what the rules are.

VERA: When was it?

MARJORIE: Just over a year ago.

VERA: I'm so sorry, Marjorie. It is so hard.

> *Beat.*

MARJORIE: Thank you.

> *MARJORIE turns to ANDRE, takes his hand.*

VERA: Why don't you go home?

MARJORIE: Uh-uh, no.

VERA: I think I need to insist.

MARJORIE:	Will someone call me if...?
VERA:	I'll leave a note for night staff.

MARJORIE stands up and gathers her belongings as THOMAS and PAULINE enter. THOMAS is giving her a tour. PAULINE is looking extremely uncomfortable. She stands in the doorway. VERA attends to ANDRE.

THOMAS:	*(As he's entering.)* ...and this is my room. 'Course they offered me the Presidential Suite, but three chandeliers is just overkill. *(Seeing MARJORIE and VERA.)* How's he doing?
VERA:	He's the same.
THOMAS:	*(Glances back at PAULINE.)* Come in. This is my sister.
VERA:	We've met.
PAULINE:	Hi, Vera.
THOMAS:	And that's Marjorie. Volunteer.
MARJORIE:	Hi.
THOMAS:	This is Pauline. And that sweet kid is named Andre.
PAULINE:	Is he okay?
THOMAS:	Um... no.

Beat. MARJORIE touches ANDRE's forehead, then exits.

THOMAS:	Bye, Marjorie. *(She's gone.)* Bathroom. Windows... with a view. Bed. This is where I'm going to meet Diana.

PAULINE: I didn't realize you shared a room.

THOMAS: Oh yeah, it's a total slumber party. Come on, I want you to meet Corey. He has the most attached earlobes I have ever seen.

PAULINE: Can't wait.

> *THOMAS exits. PAULINE pauses and takes in the room, then exits after him. VERA writes something on ANDRE's chart, then goes over and starts to adjust him in bed. ANDRE stirs. VERA pauses, then gently rocks his shoulder.*

VERA: Andre?

> *ANDRE sighs, slowly opening his eyes.*

VERA: Andre? Can you hear me? Squeeze my hand if you can... *(He squeezes.)* Hi. Hello, Andre. Are you in pain? Andre, you can squeeze my hand if you're in pain.

ANDRE: What time is it?

VERA: It's Wednesday, in the afternoon.

ANDRE: Wednesday?

VERA: Yes.

ANDRE: *(Groans.)* My back.

VERA: What's hurting?

ANDRE: It's sore. My neck. What happened?

> *VERA gathers some medication and begins to administer it.*

VERA: You were sleeping for a while. I'm going to give you something to help with the pain, okay? This should keep you relaxed.

ANDRE:	Where's Marjorie?
VERA:	She just left a second ago but she's coming back tomorrow. She's going to be so excited.
ANDRE:	My neck. This pillow.
VERA:	The meds will kick in soon.
ANDRE:	Tell her to bring my pillow from home.
VERA:	Marjorie? We've got lots of pillows here.

He groans again.

ANDRE:	Next time she goes, she can…
VERA:	Next time she goes where?
ANDRE:	To my apartment.
VERA:	To your— Marjorie has been to your apartment?
ANDRE:	It's Wednesday?
VERA:	October 23rd. Just after two p.m. Are you feeling the medication?
ANDRE:	I think so.
VERA:	Good. I'm really happy you're back with us, Andre.
ANDRE:	Same.
VERA:	I'm going to get a doctor to look you over. Rest, okay?
ANDRE:	Yeah, okay.
VERA:	I'll be right back.

VERA exits. Lights shift.

Scene 8A – The Princess Eve Suite
October 24, 1991

> *THOMAS rushes on, roaming the halls towards his room. DIANA stands in his room, listening.*

THOMAS: He was AWAKE! Oh, the relief, the relief, the relief. The hope, it returned. I couldn't sleep that entire night. Felt every single second, rehearsing my speech, checking on Andre, the ringing was back, louder and louder through the walls and the floors, and the next morning at 8:59 a.m., on the dot, it was Marco—

ANDRE: Polo.

THOMAS: Princess Eve!!! I bathed, I shaved, and then off I went to every single room, yelling "Get up! Sit up! Eat every bite of that breakfast!" It's Princess Eve!!

> *MARJORIE enters, appearing at the door and seeing that ANDRE is awake.*

MARJORIE: Andre?

ANDRE: Hi.

MARJORIE: Oh my God.

> *MARJORIE crosses to him, gives him a hug, overwhelmed with joy.*

MARJORIE: No one called me. I told them to call me.

ANDRE: It's fine, I was really out of it anyways.

MARJORIE: You're awake.

THOMAS: Princess Eve! The morning flies by, then lunch, and that afternoon...

> *PAULINE enters. THOMAS beams at her.*

PAULINE: I brought magazines!

             She holds up a magazine with the cast of 90210 on the cover.

THOMAS: Oooh, is that Luke Perry?

PAULINE: Let's go to the bench out front.

             They walk to a bench downstage.

ANDRE: Thomas said you stayed with me basically the whole time. Like even overnight.

MARJORIE: Well yeah, but don't make it sound creepy.

THOMAS: *(To PAULINE.)* Okay, I'm going to ask you something, but you cannot make a scene.

ANDRE: Marjorie, about the visit tomorrow…

THOMAS: About tomorrow…

             PAULINE gasps.

PAULINE: ARE YOU KIDDING ME?!

MARJORIE: Andre, I would be absolutely honoured.

ANDRE: I'm so nervous.

THOMAS: You can be there, but you can only say two sentences to her.

PAULINE: Four.

THOMAS: Two.

PAULINE: Three.

THOMAS: One.

PAULINE: Okay, two.

MARJORIE: Need to shave again.

ANDRE: *(Feels his face.)* I'm still pretty smooth.

MARJORIE:	I wasn't talking about you.
PAULINE:	Did you notice that I tried a different hairstyle?
THOMAS:	I noticed. Less llama-y.
PAULINE:	More poodle.
MARJORIE:	*(She shows him the bag.)* Don't make fun, but there's this witchy store near my place.
PAULINE:	I was thinking, after the Diana visit...
ANDRE:	*(Picks one up.)* Black Tourmaline.
PAULINE:	Maybe you could help me pick a new hairstyle.
MARJORIE:	You know this stuff?
ANDRE:	I love this stuff!

MARJORIE shows him the crystals.

PAULINE:	I mean come to the salon with me.
MARJORIE:	Bloodstone.
THOMAS:	Um, sure.
MARJORIE:	Bit obvious.
THOMAS:	Can we walk a bit?
PAULINE:	If you want..
MARJORIE:	*(Pulling out a stone on a chain.)* But this one's my favourite.
THOMAS:	*(To DIANA.)* PRINCESS EVE! One more sleep. Eating and standing and the beautiful ringing. And no one died.

THOMAS and PAULINE exit together, DIANA opposite.

Scene 8B — Horny Warrior

ANDRE examines the stone.

MARJORIE: Carnelian. It's supposed to be very healing.

ANDRE: *(Laughs.)* Oh my God. Carnelian is like the horny sex stone.

MARJORIE: What?

ANDRE: It's supposed to be good for, you know... sexual energy and stuff.

MARJORIE: The lady at the store said that warriors would wear it into battle. I thought it was perfect!

ANDRE: I don't know what kinda battle *they* were going to...

MARJORIE: Well, whatever. Put it on. *(He does. MARJORIE gets saucy.)* Oh, Andre. I'm suddenly feeling... so drawn to you...

ANDRE: Ew, get away.

They laugh. MARJORIE takes some stones and places them by the bed. Beat.

MARJORIE: Remember how you were talking about calling your mom?

ANDRE: Yeah.

MARJORIE: And then you didn't, and then you got super sick? I was agonizing over it the whole time. I completely talked you out of it.

ANDRE: I mean, I wasn't sure.

MARJORIE: Yes, you were. I think you should do it.

ANDRE: Really?

MARJORIE: Yes. Call her.

ANDRE: There's no point. She'd freak out on me and then be worried about everyone in my family finding out.

MARJORIE: You don't know that. And even if she does freak out, you're a warrior, for God's sake. A... horny warrior.

ANDRE: *(Laughs.)* ...Mmm, I don't know.

MARJORIE: Trust me. Call her.

ANDRE: You'd be there?

MARJORIE: I'll be right there.

ANDRE: Okay. Yeah.

> *Over the following scene, MARJORIE helps ANDRE sit up, put on a robe, and get into his wheelchair. They exit.*

Scene 8C – Semicolon

THOMAS and PAULINE on the bench.

PAULINE: Hello, Your Highness—

THOMAS: Your *Royal* Highness.

PAULINE: *I knew that!* Hello, Your Royal Highness, I am really honoured to meet you because you have been such an incredible influence on me throughout my life SEMICOLON you've supported others in admirable ways that include FULL COLON charity work COMMA being a voice for the—

THOMAS: Alright, alright.

PAULINE: That's just sentence ONE.

THOMAS: We only get a few minutes per room and Andre has to go too.

PAULINE: Right. Your roommate. *(Beat.)* Hey, question — has anyone explained to you how they decide who gets a single room and who has to share?

THOMAS: No.

PAULINE: I think it's weird, that's all.

THOMAS: I'll be sure to pass that along.

He heads to the door.

PAULINE: Wait. It's so nice. Fresh air.

She pats the bench; he sits back down.

Scene 8D – Now, Please.

> *MARJORIE and ANDRE enter downstage, arriving at the nursing station where the phone is.*

MARJORIE: Alright. How you feeling?

ANDRE: Like I'm outside my body. We haven't talked in so long. How do I even start?

MARJORIE: Something like *Hi Mom, it's Andre...*

ANDRE: And then?

MARJORIE: And then she'll either hang up or you keep talking. Maybe that's the approach—talk until she hangs up.

ANDRE: She'll get her words in if she wants to.

MARJORIE: Well, then you hang up and go meet a princess. You know the number?

ANDRE: Yes. I'm freaking out.

> *VERA enters.*

VERA: Marjorie. Can I talk to you, please?

MARJORIE: We were just about to—

VERA: Now, please.

MARJORIE: Alright. *(To ANDRE.)* I'll be right back.

ANDRE: Hurry.

> *MARJORIE exits with VERA.*

Scene 8E – Reindeer

> *THOMAS is reading the* Maclean's *now.*
> *PAULINE is eating an apple.*

PAULINE: Not to harp on this, but that boy in the room with you—

THOMAS: Andre.

PAULINE: He's very sick.

THOMAS: We're all sick.

PAULINE: What if he gets worse?

THOMAS: Then he might die.

PAULINE: And you'd be there?

THOMAS: Maybe.

PAULINE: How's that supposed to help you feel better?

THOMAS: It isn't. Although sometimes it helps *them* feel better when I'm there.

PAULINE: I mean, that shouldn't have to be your job.

THOMAS: It's not a job—

PAULINE: You should have your own room.

THOMAS: My God, you have a reindeer up your butt.

PAULINE: I don't understand it.

THOMAS: No, you can't understand it.

PAULINE: Well, I have a brain and two eyes—

THOMAS: And a disproportionately large mouth. Leave it.

> *He goes back to his magazine.*

Scene 8F – Boxes in the Basement

VERA enters with MARJORIE.

MARJORIE: If this could wait ten minutes...

VERA: Have you been going over to Andre's home?

MARJORIE: What?

VERA: Tell me the truth, please.

MARJORIE: No, of course not.

VERA: I talked to one of our property staff, who told me you brought some boxes of his stuff and put them in the basement.

MARJORIE: Well, I helped move some things.

VERA: So you have been going to his place.

MARJORIE: Just so I could get the boxes.

VERA: Do you have his house key?

Beat. MARJORIE sighs.

This crosses a line.

MARJORIE: He asked me to.

VERA: We have trained, professional social workers. There's a process.

MARJORIE: I'm sorry, I didn't know.

VERA: I think you did.

MARJORIE: No one told me.

VERA: We need to have a sit-down with Ruth.

MARJORIE: I heard you yesterday, Vera. I'm taking a step back.

VERA: Where are the house keys right now? Are they with Andre? Or in your purse?

         MARJORIE doesn't respond.

VERA: Come on.

MARJORIE: I screwed up, fine, okay, but I have got to get back to Andre.

VERA: No.

MARJORIE: Please. You're being unreasonable.

VERA: You went to his home, alone, without telling anyone! And then you just *lied* about it to my face. That's a lack of boundaries and basic goddamn respect that I can't even begin to justify. But what *really* worries me is that you don't even seem to understand why any of this is a problem. This can't wait a minute. Let's go.

         MARJORIE exits, VERA follows.
         Upstage, ANDRE sits nervously, waiting.

Scene 8G – Whoosh

THOMAS stands up.

THOMAS: Alright, nap time.

PAULINE: Should I come back tonight?

THOMAS: If it's not too late for your advanced age.

THOMAS starts to head inside.

PAULINE: Wait... Thomas.

THOMAS: Yeah?

PAULINE: Move in with me.

THOMAS: *(Laughs.)* In Scarborough?

PAULINE: Yes.

THOMAS: What? Why?

PAULINE: So I can take care of you.

THOMAS: I'm okay here, thanks.

PAULINE: You aren't.

THOMAS: Um, yes, I am.

PAULINE: You have no privacy. You share a bathroom.

THOMAS: Oh, there are multiple toilets in your basement suite?

PAULINE: No, but I'm your sister. Those are strangers.

THOMAS: They're not strangers.

PAULINE: Practically.

THOMAS: You don't really know what you're talking about.

PAULINE: Well, I know that Vera's kind of a bitch.

THOMAS: Vera's the best nurse I have ever met..

PAULINE: Move in with me. It'll be like before.

THOMAS: I know you're trying to be nice. But no.

PAULINE: You're being dumb about this. I can take care of you. I've been doing it since forever.

THOMAS: You have not.

PAULINE: Oh, come on.

THOMAS: No. Discussion over.

PAULINE: Why not?

THOMAS: Because I live here!

PAULINE: But why would you if you don't have to?

THOMAS: It's my home now.

PAULINE: This isn't a home.

THOMAS: It's MY home! *(He gets up and paces, irate.)* It's the ONE good thing! Your guilt doesn't get to undermine the ONE GOOD THING I have!

PAULINE: It's not guilt! You could get better!

THOMAS: Oh my God, you're still not— Just saying that *shows* that you're not—!

         THOMAS becomes unstable on his feet.

THOMAS: Oh shit. I'm really— oh shit— Help me sit— Pauline—!

         He reaches for PAULINE, who instinctively recoils from his touch, causing him to lurch forwards, trip, and violently fall to the ground.

PAULINE: Oh my God! Tommy!

THOMAS: Ah shit shit shit.

PAULINE: Are you okay?

THOMAS: GET HELP!

PAULINE: *(Calls out:)* HELP! CAN SOMEONE HELP?

> *THOMAS has hit his head. He feels a bump and looks at his hand. There is some blood. PAULINE shrinks back.*

PAULINE: Oh God. You're, um... you're gonna be okay...

> *VERA enters.*

VERA: What is going on—?

> *She sees THOMAS and rushes to him.*

VERA: Thomas—

PAULINE: He lost his balance and fell.

> *As VERA goes to examine him:*

PAULINE: He's bleeding. He's bleeding!

THOMAS: I'm fine.

VERA: Let me look.

THOMAS: Help me feel better, she says. She wants to help me feel better.

PAULINE: I do—

THOMAS: Help YOURSELF feel better!

VERA: Okay now. Deep breaths.

PAULINE: I am trying to be there for you.

THOMAS: By disappearing on me—

VERA: Do you feel dizzy?

THOMAS: No, not at all.

PAULINE: He hit his head.

THOMAS: I am FINE! Let me get up, for God's sake.

VERA: Slowly. In the moment.

              THOMAS is up and stable.

THOMAS: Just get me away from her.

PAULINE: Tommy—

THOMAS: How do you think you could help take care of me if you can't even touch me?

              VERA and THOMAS start exiting. DIANA enters.

PAULINE: Please, Tommy—

THOMAS: *(Stops, out to DIANA:)* Whoosh.

Scene 9 – Alone
That evening

> *ANDRE is sitting in the common room,
> alone. MARJORIE enters.*

MARJORIE: Oh, you're in here. I was heading up to your room. *(ANDRE doesn't reply.)* I heard about Thomas. Is he okay?

ANDRE: Sleeping.

MARJORIE: Sorry it took so long. Should we go call your mom?

ANDRE: Where were you?

MARJORIE: Vera found out about me going to your house. Ruth is pissed, they've given me an "official warning" and the choice between kitchen duty or going home.

ANDRE: I was waiting.

MARJORIE: I couldn't sneak away. Let's go now.

ANDRE: I already called her.

MARJORIE: What? You did?

ANDRE: I was losing my mind.

MARJORIE: What happened?

> *ANDRE shrugs, looks out the window.*

…What?

ANDRE: The number is out of service.

MARJORIE: Oh.

ANDRE: I never should have called. At least before I could imagine that someone was thinking about me.

MARJORIE: I'm sure your family still thinks of you.

ANDRE: You don't change your number if you want someone to call. I am never, ever going to speak to my mom again. That's it forever.

MARJORIE: I'm so sorry.

ANDRE: ARE YOU?

MARJORIE: WHAT? You know I would have been there.

ANDRE: You weren't.

MARJORIE: Honey, you should have waited—

ANDRE: What difference would that have made?

MARJORIE: You wouldn't have been alone.

ANDRE: I am alone. I've known you for a week.

Long pause.

ANDRE: Is this what you were hoping would happen?

MARJORIE: What do you mean?

ANDRE: When you forced me to call her?

MARJORIE: You wanted to call her.

Beat.

I… No. Andre.

Beat. No answer.

Jesus. I'm just trying to help.

ANDRE: Who's helping who?

                    *ANDRE starts to wheel himself out of the
                    room. MARJORIE goes to push him.*

ANDRE: I didn't ask.

                    *MARJORIE takes a step back. ANDRE
                    exits, leaving MARJORIE alone on stage.
                    Shift.*

Scene 10 – Ficus
The same night

> *VERA is at the nursing station, working. PAULINE enters.*

PAULINE: Is he any better?

VERA: I thought you left.

PAULINE: No.

VERA: He's resting.

PAULINE: Can I just say goodnight?

VERA: I don't think that's a good idea.

PAULINE: I need to speak to someone about his room.

VERA: What about his room?

PAULINE: I don't understand why he has to share. How is that decided?

VERA: There are considerations.

PAULINE: Well, I want to speak to someone about it.

VERA: Alright.

PAULINE: And I have a few other concerns.

VERA: Fine. I'll have someone call you.

> *MARJORIE enters.*

PAULINE: I want to know, if someone is still here—alive and walking—five months later, why were they admitted in the first place?

MARJORIE: *(To VERA.)* I'm just getting my coat.

PAULINE: Are you listening to me?

VERA:	Yes.
PAULINE:	He's in a dark, tiny room with a stranger, eating in his bed and sharing a bathroom. How does any of that lead to getting him better?
VERA:	It doesn't.
PAULINE:	Oh, so you admit it.

VERA begins to leave.

VERA:	Someone will call you.
PAULINE:	How can you be so cold? I'm talking to you.
MARJORIE:	I'd save your breath.
PAULINE:	Honestly, it's inhumane the way she—

VERA stops in her tracks.

VERA:	Jesus. I'm just trying to do my fucking job.
MARJORIE:	Apparently feelings aren't part of the job description.

Beat.

VERA:	*(To MARJORIE.)* You never answered the question.
MARJORIE:	What question?
PAULINE:	I think I want to file a formal complaint.
VERA:	Please do. I'll lick the envelope. Marjorie, why do you want to volunteer here? It's not a trick. Just tell me why.
MARJORIE:	To help men with AIDS.

VERA:	To help them what?
MARJORIE:	I know why I came here.
PAULINE:	Is she like this with everyone?
VERA:	To help them what?
MARJORIE:	You may feel special because you work here but I have been very connected to this community for a long time, dear.
VERA:	Thomas always jokes that Jacob was my favourite. *(To PAULINE.)* That was his last roommate. Marjorie knew him for a bit, but that was actually his second admission. He was here for longer before, just over three months. It was impossible not to like him. He completely disarmed me. In about two seconds it was three months later, and we were very close. And he was doing a lot better. Night and day. I thought... maybe he's one of the few that gets out and lives for a few more years. So he got discharged, and he got a place and I went to visit him a couple times a week and he was doing great. I bought him a houseplant. Now, any guesses what happened next?
MARJORIE:	He died. I was there.
VERA:	Before that. One day I showed up at his place and he was on the ground, where he'd been, alone, for five hours. I got him an ambulance and brought him back here. But it wasn't like before. The disappointment was worse than any pain. And I became his sworn enemy. He called me every name you can think of, but when he said, "I hate you..."
MARJORIE:	He didn't actually hate you.

VERA:	He hated that he'd been allowed to think that there was any sort of escape. And I facilitated that. I bought him a stupid plant. As if he could outlive a ficus. And then he was disappointed, and then he was dead. And I... had four more hours left in my shift.
MARJORIE:	You have to think about what you contributed—
VERA:	We are here to help men with AIDS. We are here to help them die. It is a huge gift to give, and it is enough. Any confusion about that — trust me, trust me — will only cause pain.
MARJORIE:	I think you can help someone die and help them live at the same time.
VERA:	Yeah. Once in your lifetime, maybe. Twice if you're really, really strong.
MARJORIE:	I need to talk to Andre.

MARJORIE exits towards the room. Beat.

PAULINE:	Do you think my brother hates me?
VERA:	I think he's a lot more scared than he lets on.
PAULINE:	Because he's going to die.
VERA:	Yes.
PAULINE:	So what can I do?
VERA:	Help him die.
PAULINE:	I don't know how to do that.
VERA:	You will.

MARJORIE rushes back onstage.

MARJORIE:	Vera, you need to come. Now.

PAULINE: What's wrong?

MARJORIE: Vera.

VERA: Wait here.

PAULINE: I want to see him.

VERA: Wait.

> *MARJORIE and VERA exit. PAULINE waits at the nursing station.*

Scene 11 – Popsicles and Princesses

> *In the bedroom with ANDRE and THOMAS. THOMAS is sitting on his bed, talking to himself, agitated. ANDRE is sitting up in his bed, worried.*

THOMAS: There's so much to get done. How can you honestly think that it's all going to be done on time?

ANDRE: Don't worry, it'll get done.

THOMAS: It won't. Might as well give up.

ANDRE: It will, I promise.

THOMAS: How can you be sure!?!

ANDRE: Someone told me.

THOMAS: Who?! Vera?

ANDRE: Don't worry about it.

THOMAS: Do you think I'm stupid?

> *THOMAS gets up, walks around the room.*

ANDRE: No. No no—

THOMAS: Look at this place! It's a mess in here. These books just thrown in the corner, garbages unemptied. Disgusting.

ANDRE: No look, they're empty. They're all empty. And the cleaners are coming tomorrow.

THOMAS: Tomorrow?! Tomorrow?! That's too late, for God's sake. *(He rubs his arm.)* My arm is so itchy.

ANDRE: Thomas, why don't you get back into bed?

THOMAS: Why don't you go back to bed? Why don't you get me a Popsicle and then go back to bed?

ANDRE: You want a Popsicle?

THOMAS: I'm so thirsty and my arm is like, it's like there are fire ants crawling all over it.

VERA enters, followed by MARJORIE.

VERA: Hi, Thomas. How you doing?

THOMAS: Oh, thank God, finally. Look at this place.

VERA: What about it?

THOMAS: It's a disaster in here!

ANDRE: He's very worried that we're not prepared for the royal visit.

THOMAS: Well, aren't you? Isn't everyone?! What, is the Princess to have to clear clothing off a chair before being allowed to sit?

ANDRE: It's not a mess in here.

VERA: Of course not.

MARJORIE: Thomas, there's still lots of time before—

VERA: What would you like me to tidy? I'll tidy it and you get back into bed.

THOMAS: Well, all those papers over there. Boxes and bags. And what is that smell?

MARJORIE: I'll open a window.

THOMAS: And all of these clothes that have been— Jesus, it's obvious, you idiot. If it's out of place then put it away, idiot.

VERA:	Sure. Marjorie, how about you get Andre in his chair and take him to the common room for a while?
THOMAS:	Good.
VERA:	And I'll take care of everything.

MARJORIE helps ANDRE into his chair. VERA moves the books.

THOMAS:	No. You go find my sister.
VERA:	Are you sure?
THOMAS:	Of course I'm sure! Go!

VERA exits.

THOMAS:	Well, his sheets are getting everywhere. You're making it worse, you idiot.
MARJORIE:	I'm sorry.
ANDRE:	Thomas, just calm down okay?
THOMAS:	How can you tell me to calm down?!! And how are you not more worried!?!?
ANDRE:	It's all going to get figured out.
THOMAS:	By who? You bunch of assholes?
MARJORIE:	We're all going to work together.
THOMAS:	What are you even—?

PAULINE enters.

VERA:	Here she is.
PAULINE:	Thomas, I—

THOMAS gasps. Pause.

THOMAS:	Oh my God.
VERA:	Everything okay?
THOMAS:	Of course. *(THOMAS bows his head to PAULINE.)* Your Royal Highness. It's an honour.

Silence. For a moment, everyone is still.

VERA:	Why don't you get into bed?
THOMAS:	Yes. Is that how it's done?
PAULINE:	Well, I…
VERA:	Exactly. Get into bed and I'll get you comfortable. *(To ANDRE and MARJORIE:)* You should go. Give them some privacy.

ANDRE and MARJORIE exit. THOMAS crosses to his bed.

THOMAS:	Terribly underdressed for the occasion, of course, but then you wouldn't care about anything like that, would you?
VERA:	Of course she doesn't.
PAULINE:	Not at all.

THOMAS is in bed.

THOMAS:	There. All set.
VERA:	Good.

Long beat. VERA considers, then looks to PAULINE, asking for her trust.

Your Highness, I would like to formally introduce you to Thomas.

THOMAS:	*(Laughs.)* I'm really nervous.

PAULINE: So am I.

VERA: Should I leave you then, or would you like me to—?

THOMAS: Could you find my sister, please?

VERA: I'll look for her.

THOMAS: Good.

> *THOMAS raises his hand towards PAULINE, expectantly. There's a pause. PAULINE looks to VERA.*

THOMAS: Oh, I'm sorry. That was too forward. I was told you touch people.

VERA: I'm sure it was okay. There's just protocol, so—

> *PAULINE crosses the room. She takes THOMAS' hand.*

PAULINE: Thank you.

VERA: Alright.

> *VERA crosses and sits to the side. There is a pause. THOMAS lifts PAULINE's hand to his face and rubs it against his cheek. PAULINE runs her other hand down his arm and touches his chest. They touch foreheads and smile.*

THOMAS: Here we are at last.

PAULINE: At last.

Scene 12 — Semi-consciousness

> *The lights shift dramatically. The world of the play enters a state of semi-consciousness. DIANA enters.*

THOMAS: I know it's stupid to start with, but I want you to know that I watched every single minute of your wedding. My sister and I. My sister and I. *(Laughs.)* Five a.m., which she hated. We watched... long ride, were you...? Wishing that moment away down the... tree-lined, long long, it's so long. And then you're laughing, and then you're... blowing softly in the... the...Whoosh.

PAULINE/
DIANA: I'm here.

THOMAS: You're here. At last. That dress.

PAULINE: My funeral dress?

DIANA: *(Over PAULINE.)* The Emanuels.

THOMAS: You're not wearing that, are you? Hate that stupid...

PAULINE/
DIANA: Shhh...

THOMAS: I'm sick. I'm not feeling good. Stupid. Awful. How could you do this to me? You disappointment.

PAULINE: I'm sorry. I'm so sorry. Shh shhh, I'm here now.

DIANA: *(Over PAULINE.)* People are scared of the illness; not the person.

THOMAS: Head exploding. Neck, back. Knee, ankle, foot.

DIANA:	All the tiny simple things…
THOMAS:	Please, seven, please, make it. Please let me…
PAULINE:	You're gonna make it.
DIANA:	*(Over PAULINE.)* You can make it.
THOMAS:	I'm really nervous. Will you hold my hand?
DIANA:	She is holding your hand.

> *THOMAS looks at his hand, then up to PAULINE.*

THOMAS:	Pauline?
PAULINE:	Tommy.
THOMAS:	I'm so glad you're here.
PAULINE:	Yeah. And I'm not going anywhere. *(Steel Magnolias:)* "I love ya more than my luggage."
THOMAS:	*(Laughs.)* "I love ya more than my luggage." *(Beat. He looks at her anew.)* Hello, Pauline.
PAULINE:	Hello—

> *THOMAS' eyes grow heavy. He settles his head into the pillow.*

PAULINE:	Wait, stay here.
THOMAS:	I think I'll close my eyes…

> *THOMAS lowers down in bed. PAULINE glances at VERA, who gives her a nod.*

PAULINE:	Okay.
THOMAS:	Keep holding my hand.
PAULINE:	For-fucking-ever.

THOMAS: Thank you. *(He settles into his pillow.)* Your train stretched on and on… leaving a mark that you were there… blowing softly in the wind.

              The lights have gradually shifted back to the normal room lighting. THOMAS drifts off to sleep while PAULINE sits and holds his hand and VERA stands by.

Scene 13 – Crying in the Bath
October 25, 1991

> *ANDRE is sitting at a window on the second floor, looking out at the gathering crowd. MARJORIE enters.*

MARJORIE: A lot of people out there.

ANDRE: Yeah, there are.

MARJORIE: There's a better view in Leonard's room.

ANDRE: I know. He keeps reminding everyone.

> *Beat.*

MARJORIE: I was, uh… Remember I told you about Michael? My best… —Well I had a little chat with him last night. In my head, obviously. Well, actually he was in my head, I was talking out loud. In the bath. Because you don't need Kleenex if you cry in the bath. He reminded me of something he said once when half of my classroom failed an exam and I was in shit with my boss. He said: *They don't need a friend, Marj, they need someone to teach them goddamn grammar.* I guess it's a pattern.

ANDRE: Okay.

MARJORIE: I'm sorry. *(Beat.)* I think maybe I came here too soon.

ANDRE: *(Coldly.)* I'm glad I could help you figure that out.

MARJORIE: *(She nods.)* I'm finishing the week and then going to go… do something else. I'd like to visit you, but obviously that's up to you. Anyways, I'll leave you alone. Big day. Exciting.

MARJORIE goes to leave.

ANDRE: Can you still be there during the visit?

              MARJORIE is stopped dead. A beat.

MARJORIE: You want that?

ANDRE: It's that or be alone.

MARJORIE: Of course.

ANDRE: Thanks.

              ANDRE exits.

Scene 14 – The Big Day
Later that day

> *A flurry of activity. THOMAS is in bed, ANDRE in his wheelchair beside his bed. VERA, MARJORIE, and PAULINE do some final preparations in the room. VERA exits as PAULINE takes position next to THOMAS, MARJORIE next to ANDRE.*

VERA: Now may I introduce Andre and his friend Marjorie—

DIANA: Hello.

> *They nod their heads and MARJORIE does a self-conscious half-curtsy.*

VERA: And this is Thomas and his sister Pauline.

PAULINE: It's a pleasure to meet you, your Highne—... Your Royal Highness.

DIANA: It's all my pleasure.

> *DIANA crosses to THOMAS and PAULINE.*

DIANA: May I?

PAULINE: Please.

> *DIANA takes THOMAS' hand.*

DIANA: For how long has he been in a coma?

PAULINE: Since yesterday. He was so excited about meeting you.

DIANA: Well, he's meeting me now. Hello, Thomas, it's a pleasure.

PAULINE: That's where he would probably have made some awkward joke about not being appropriately dressed.

DIANA: I think he looks marvellous.

PAULINE: He loves you so much.

DIANA: Would you tell me about him?

PAULINE: He... Well he is... My brother is one of the most... *(Brimming with pain and sadness.)* Sorry.

VERA: Thomas is one of the funniest people I've ever had the pleasure of working with.

DIANA: Yes, I can see the sense of humour around his eyes.

MARJORIE: And honest.

PAULINE: Sometimes a bit too honest.

DIANA: That's a bit of a gift and a curse, isn't it?

PAULINE: There were a lot of things he wanted to say but I can't... I don't know where to—

DIANA takes PAULINE's hand, too. ANDRE takes MARJORIE's hand, they look at each other. Everyone is still. A silence.

DIANA: There. It was nice to meet you, Thomas.

She replaces his hand on his chest.

ANDRE: There was a question he wanted to ask.

DIANA: Yes?

ANDRE: He said it would sound dumb, but that it'd be the perfect icebreaker and you'd have the exact perfect answer.

DIANA: What was it?

ANDRE looks to VERA and MARJORIE. They smile.

ANDRE: What are you going to be for Halloween?

Scene 15 – Thomas and Diana

There's a transition. The stage darkens. It's night. PAULINE sits by THOMAS' bed, reading. ANDRE sits up in his bed, writing in his journal. VERA and MARJORIE are at the nursing station. THOMAS sits up in bed. DIANA crosses in front of him, exiting.

THOMAS: *(To DIANA.)* So that's it then? Off you go?

DIANA: You can come with me if you like. Or not.

THOMAS: What, and stay here all alone?

DIANA: You don't look alone to me.

THOMAS: No. *(Beat.)* Now? *(He takes a deep breath in and closes his eyes. Beat. He opens them.)* No.

DIANA turns and starts exiting again.

THOMAS: Wait, I'm coming. Or no, never mind. It's not what I was expecting.

DIANA: What were you expecting?

THOMAS: I don't know. A bit of grandeur, for God's sake. Harp music? Reflection? Absolution. That's not a thing, is it? Maybe I'm doing it wrong. *(He closes his eyes.)* A long road. And a carriage. Thousands of people standing on either side of the street, cheering me along. Thousands. Thousands. Thousands. Do you take in that moment? Or wish it would just happen already? *(He takes a deep breath in. Beat. He opens his eyes and sighs.)* Vera's always telling me to take a moment. Take it day by day, take a moment, take in the moment, take take take. Take a breath. *(Inhales, closes his eyes.)* If you think about it, living is inhaling. To live is to take a breath. Which means… exhaling is… dying is…

> *THOMAS opens his eyes, struck by a realization. He's scared to breathe out.*

DIANA: Giving. Give over. Give in.

THOMAS: Give. Give your memory. Give your love away. Forgive. Give vibrations. Give light like a candle in the window. Give up?

DIANA: Yes, in a way.

THOMAS: Give yourself. Give yourself over to those who deserve to keep you. Death is an exhale. Death... is giving.

> *He takes a deep, painful breath, holds for a terrified second, then:*

Whoosh.

> *Everyone onstage shifts subtly as THOMAS' spirit passes through, becoming forever a part of who they are. THOMAS stands.*

Wait. *(Steel Magnolias:)* "The only thing that separates us from the animals is our ability to accessorize."

My carriage is here. My train is flowing. I'm ready to walk.

> *As THOMAS walks, a long, white train made of bedsheets trails behind him from the bed, stretching on and on and on as he walks towards DIANA and his death.*

> *Lights out.*

> *The End.*

Laura Condlln as Pauline, Stratford Festival, 2023. Directed by Andrew Kushnir. Designed by Joshua Quinlan. Lighting designed by Louise Guinand. Photo by Cylla Von Tiedemann. Photo courtesy of the Stratford Festival.

From left: Laura Condlln as Pauline, Sean Arbuckle as Thomas, and Krystin Pellerin as Diana, Stratford Festival, 2023. Directed by Andrew Kushnir. Designed by Joshua Quinlan. Lighting designed by Louise Guinand. Photo by Cylla Von Tiedemann. Photo courtesy of the Stratford Festival.

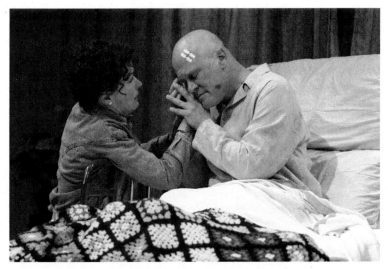

Laura Condlln as Pauline and Sean Arbuckle as Thomas, Stratford Festival, 2023. Directed by Andrew Kushnir. Designed by Joshua Quinlan. Lighting designed by Louise Guinand. Photo by Cylla Von Tiedemann. Photo courtesy of the Stratford Festival.

Sean Arbuckle as Thomas and Krystin Pellerin as Diana, Stratford Festival, 2023. Directed by Andrew Kushnir. Designed by Joshua Quinlan. Lighting designed by Louise Guinand. Photo by Cylla Von Tiedemann. Photo courtesy of the Stratford Festival.

Afterword: Reflections on *Casey and Diana*

Nancy Roe-Lucier

Nick Green's play, *Casey and Diana*, brings to light an important time during the AIDS pandemic when there was so much stigma surrounding the disease. The play tells a fictional story, yet it captures the true sentiment and profound impact that Princess Diana's visit had on everyone who was part of that day.

I had the privilege of being with my dad at Casey House to meet Princess Diana, along with one of my sisters. It was a thrilling moment in our lives. The royal visit carried my family through a very difficult time when we had just learned that our dad had AIDS. It was exciting when her visit was announced, and we were briefly able to shift our focus from pain and heartache to what our time with the princess would be like. Growing up in a family that adored the British Royals, meeting Princess Diana was beyond our imagination.

I saw the première of *Casey and Diana* at the Stratford Festival with my three adult children. It was a very emotional and touching experience to be there together. The play provided a window into Casey House as it was at the time of Princess Diana's visit, and my children were better able to understand what it may have been like for me, going to visit my dad and struggling as he was dying. It shows the excitement and anticipation surrounding the royal visit, as well as the difficult realities of isolation and loneliness that clients of the hospice faced.

Princess Diana's presence was magical, and she greeted my dad with complete acceptance. She was interested in his care and wanted to know what it was like for him living at Casey House. I had the chance to tell her I had made scrapbooks of her royal wedding when I was younger. Her warmth lingered with us, and my dad's health and spirits improved for a short period following her visit. She had a meaningful impact by giving us something positive to talk about in the difficult months ahead. We had shared a bond of something extraordinary. Princess Diana's visit strengthened our ability to face any stigma around HIV. To this day, I bring out my photos with her and it sparks a whole new conversation.

Casey House staff embraced my family with dignity and compassion, providing much-needed support through my dad's end of life care. We witnessed and learned from their dedication, expertise, care and generosity of human spirit. In this place of peace and acceptance, my dad was able to have a dignified death. My siblings and I experienced hope, kindness and resiliency at Casey House, and Princess Diana's visit played such an important part in our journey.

Casey and Diana took me back to a moment in time that had such a lasting impact in my life. It recreates the homelike setting of exceptional bedside care and the warmth of Casey House, symbolized by the stained-glass windows. It's an emotional story that, from my experience, captures the fear, heartache, compassion and resolution surrounding those dying at Casey House in the early years of the AIDS pandemic.

Thank you, Nick Green for *Casey and Diana,* and for opening the conversation for shared stories of those who have been touched by Casey House and Princess Diana's visit. I am deeply grateful.

Erika Epprecht
Casey House nurse, 1988–2022

I recall the anticipation of Diana's visit as quite an exciting time. It felt like a special day to look forward to, a bright beacon of light to be cast upon us! I value the humanitarian experience of working as a registered nurse at Casey House during those formative years and the caring and compassionate culture embraced by the organization and staff. However, within that realm of care, we were witness to much suffering, sadness and loss.

I was not scheduled to work the day of Diana's visit. Nonetheless, the event was not to be missed! Non-working staff were also invited to attend and assigned designated waiting areas. Much of the nursing staff were excitedly bundled together in the nursing station.

Prior to her arrival, several of us were watching from the upstairs lounge window which faced the Isabella and Huntley corner. A small, enthusiastic crowd was gathering there. There were people in wheelchairs and I believe several came from the nearby now-defunct Wellesley Hospital. People cheered as her limo arrived. I recall noting how quickly she was out of her car and off out amongst the welcoming crowd. People were so happy as she greeted them. It was fascinating to watch her interact and to witness the joy. I remember thinking "Wow, she is so good at her job. She is so good in this role she does, she is such a professional!"

I am not privy to Diana's tour of Casey House, but I understand she goes room to room and greets the residents individually. We await our moment in the nursing station located on the second floor. Here she comes! She chats briefly with us, I don't recall the words, but I do recall the laughter. I was too star-struck to speak. I am dressed up for the occasion wearing my favourite black jacket and earrings to celebrate. Diana bent down for the group photo as she was quite a bit taller and we were able to gather around her. The photo captures the smiling and dazzled staff. It was fun.

And then she was gone, off to her next visit that day. As the play portrays, it was an important day for Casey House and the HIV community. She shone her celebrity spotlight upon us and that day we received global notice for the valuable work and lives at Casey House. She demonstrated to the world that people living with HIV/AIDS also deserved love and care. Her advocacy enlightened and educated many at a time when fear and stigma were rife. We had been recognized and her notice felt both genuine and gratefully supportive. And then, we carried on.

Richard Silver
Former Casey House Board Member

Volunteering at Casey House Hospice in its early years was an experience that profoundly shaped my understanding of compassion and human dignity. Guided by the remarkable June Callwood, we navigated uncharted territories, as there were no pre-existing models for an AIDS hospice. Each day presented new challenges and opportunities to innovate in care and empathy.

My journey towards understanding the profound impact of AIDS began through personal loss. I witnessed three friends succumb to the disease, each experience painfully distinct. The first loss occurred in a hospital setting, where my friend was isolated, his last days marked by a heart-wrenching absence of family and a clinical barrier of gowns and masks. The second experience was even more harrowing, in a U.S. hospital where another friend was denied even the basic comfort of morphine. His doctor's rationale — that it would adversely affect his medical outlook — was both illogical and inhumane, considering he was in his final hours.

However, it was the third experience, at Casey House Hospice, that redefined the end-of-life journey for those with AIDS. Here, my friend's last days were transformed into what June Callwood aptly described as a "velvet experience." The hospice was a sanctuary where dignity, care, and compassion were paramount, a stark contrast to the previous experiences of isolation and neglect.

One of the most impactful moments during my time at Casey House was the visit by Princess Diana. She moved through the hospice like a beacon of hope and understanding. Her approach—speaking directly, warmly, and without gloves to each resident—was revolutionary at a time when misinformation and fear surrounded AIDS. Her actions spoke volumes, demonstrating a profound empathy and a desire to connect with those suffering.

Yet, the moment that truly resonated with me was when Princess Diana interacted with a hearing-impaired family member of a resident. As a nurse began to translate the conversation into sign language, Diana intuitively paused and communicated directly in sign language. This gesture transcended mere words; it was an act of profound respect and understanding, acknowledging the individual's needs and humanity.

These experiences at Casey House, under the guidance of June and with the inspiring presence of figures like Princess Diana, were not just about providing care. They were about changing perceptions, breaking down barriers, and advocating for the dignity of those who were often marginalized and misunderstood. This journey has been one of the greatest honours of my life, teaching me invaluable lessons about compassion, advocacy, and the power of human connection in facing some of life's most challenging moments.

Photo courtesy of Casey House Collection.